UNCLE MARK'S
AMAZING ADVENTURES

 The Lyrics of a Unificationist's Life

MARK HANLON

This book is a work of non-fiction. Unless otherwise noted, the author and the publisher make no explicit guarantees as to the accuracy of the information contained in this book and in some cases, names of people and places have been altered to protect their privacy.

LifeRich Publishing is a registered trademark of The Reader's Digest Association, Inc.

LifeRich Publishing books may be ordered through booksellers or by contacting:

LifeRich Publishing
1663 Liberty Drive
Bloomington, IN 47403
www.liferichpublishing.com
1 (888) 238-8637

Because of the dynamic nature of the Internet, any web addresses or links contained in this book may have changed since publication and may no longer be valid. The views expressed in this work are solely those of the author and do not necessarily reflect the views of the publisher, and the publisher hereby disclaims any responsibility for them.

ISBN: 978-1-4897-1744-3 (sc)
ISBN: 978-1-4897-1743-6 (hc)
ISBN: 978-1-4897-1745-0 (e)

Library of Congress Control Number: 2018905955

Print information available on the last page.

LifeRich Publishing rev. date: 06/11/2018

CONTENTS

PROLOGUE

But, Oh, the music that I heard a-seeping through the
Bridegroom's door;
The cymbal and the harp all joined in praise.
The smell of new wine like on earth there's none,
Fresh venison and more;
But most of all I saw the Bridegroom's face.
                    "The Bridegroom's Face" by Sandra Lowen

azing back at the Knife's Edge and Baxter Peak, the five of us sat speechless for nearly an hour. The physical and emotional roller coaster of climbing Katahdin and walking across the precarious mile long trail was not what I had signed up for. We collapsed there exhausted, spent by 9 hours of walking, climbing and scooting across fractured granite and scaling vertical crevasses. A feeling of satisfaction gradually set in and began to warm our hearts and spirits as we relaxed and watched the sun set far in the west, 200 miles away in the White Mountains of neighboring New Hampshire. The final peaceful summit on which we rested is called Pamola, the name of a sometimes angry bird spirit of the Abenaki Indians. As we slowly soaked in the reality of what we just accomplished, I realized how little faith and trust I had. I thought of the thousands of steps and boulders we had traversed to get to this point. I had said quite a few things along the way to Ray that I regretted, but in the end, I was so grateful that he had brought me along. I looked back at the terrifying jagged trail between Baxter and Pamola and hoped that someday I would do it again, only next time with a different attitude.

It started out as an easy walk through the woods, gently climbing up to Chimney Pond. A huge male moose had walked within a few feet of us on his way to his favorite lake to forage its bottom. As we passed through the virgin timber of Baxter State Park, I felt very small and insignificant in comparison to the ancient towering white pines, their branches and needles obscuring the looming mass of rock in the distance. After three hours, we stood on the shore of the pond and looked up at the imposing, black, mile high monolith that is called Mt. Katahdin. Even in mid-July there were a few patches of snow in the crevasses. The jagged Knife's Edge was reflected in the crystal clear water, the peaceful scene belied the harrowing climb we were about to experience.

As we began the ascent of Cathedral Trail, we realized this was not going to be a walk so much as a climb. Pulling ourselves up with our hands and stepping up ledge after ledge, we were quickly gaining in altitude. The trail is nothing more than a mile-high pile of rocks. Finding hand holds was difficult in places and impossible if not for the markings painted on the faces of the stones. Up and up we went, higher and higher, rock by rock. Just when we thought we were near the top, there was another thousand feet more, then another thousand and then another. Finally, we reached the summit, arms and legs weary from the three hours of exertion. Taking in the amazing view from the Atlantic Ocean to Boston to the White Mountains, we felt like we were at the top of the world. Looking back though, we realized there was no way we were going to get down that same trail. There was only one way down and that was across the precarious, 1.1-mile-long, Knife's Edge. Looking across the Knife's Edge I suddenly realized that I was in way over my head. I'm not a mountain climber, but a musician with a healthy fear of heights. When my friend Ray told me about Katahdin, he described it as a beautiful place and awesome mountain that had a narrow trail that was high but did not require special equipment. All of that is true, but …

As we started down the trail the path was about three feet wide and straight down on both sides. I looked down at Chimney Pond. From 5,267 feet Chimney Pond appeared as a puddle. The huge white pines were now mere blades of grass. What was a calm clear 80 degrees was now forty with wind gusts over 30 mph. We were far above the tree line. I looked down on the few clouds below. Occasionally snow would blow up the northern face of the mountain and hit us in the chin. Imagine a roller coaster put on top of such a mountain. That's what we were about to climb over. The trail quickly narrowed to at times 6 inches wide and several thousand feet straight down on either side. We came across a marker which read so and so fell from this spot in the 1940s. After a while we passed another one that marked the spot where a group of people had frozen to death.

We continued following the yellow markers until we reached a point that was so narrow and gnarly that it was not possible to go up over the top. The markers led us down off to the left where they abruptly ended at the near vertical stone wall. We could see that the only way to continue was to traverse perhaps 15 feet of vertical cliff face across a granite shelf not quite as wide as the length of my shoe. There were absolutely no hand holds and you had to literally put your nose against the face of the mountain to keep from falling backwards. This is the point I began to swear. I told Ray that I wasn't sure how I was going to get down but that when I did I was going to kill him for sure. Each of us slowly scooted across the ledge.

Having accomplished this, we then saw a wildly narrow jagged saw tooth section. It was possible to walk across it but you really couldn't stand up but rather crouch down to keep your balance, sometimes on all fours or straddling the entire mountain with legs dangling on either side. I really could not look down. Eventually we came to a spot where the trail ended at a crevasse perhaps 200 feet straight down and straight up the other side. The only way across was to jump a length which was perhaps a little longer than a normal step. It was like something out of Raiders of the Lost Ark. The problem was you had to stand up and run perhaps 10 feet and jump across. My legs at this point felt like jello. It took a few more swears at Ray and I was across. That left us with one final challenge, the Chimney, a vertical rock formation which can only be described as climbing down into and out of a well with no water at the bottom. Finally, we reached Pamola. There were at that point perhaps 50 people who had traversed the Knife's Edge that day. Pamola produces an instant state of meditation for all who cross the Knife's Edge. 50 people perched on rocks in total silence, watching the sun go down on Katahdin, the great mountain.

As I write this book, I feel as I did on Pamola that day in the summer of 1976, having completed an amazing unexpected adventure. Katahdin was in a way a precursor to my journey. My story really begins a few months later, in the fall of 1976. It is an adventure full of impossible, painful situations, exhilarations, fears, joys and revelations. It was at times dangerous or lonely, but always with markers leading the way, teaching me to trust in God, myself and a few good friends. I can't complain about it. It was after all, my choice.

INTRODUCTION

M ost of my friends and relatives call me Uncle Mark. For many years my wife, Ursula and I could not have children. During that time my friends, most of whom were like my brothers and sisters, afforded me the title "uncle" out of respect. Their children naturally called me Uncle Mark. Somehow the title has stuck.

I am not a spiritual person per se. I enjoy normal things like baseball, hanging out with friends and jammin' some AC/DC or the Beatles with my musical buddies. I like pizza, Star Trek reruns and taking my sweetheart to the movies. I have no interest in theological dialogue. I would rather talk about Deflategate than salvation. I don't care how many angels can float on the head of a pin. Though I was at one time an evangelist at this point I am not trying to convert anyone. If you happen to have religious beliefs that differ from mine I suggest you keep yours. I'm not preaching to you.

I am not forcing my beliefs or friendship on anyone. I gave up on that a long time ago. I am only going to tell you what I experienced. I leave it up to you to determine what it means, if anything. If you like me a little less because of reading this, I am sorry. The story is not about me. It's about telling the truth. It's about how God worked in the life of one unsuspecting, unprepared kid from New England. It's the good, the bad, the beautiful and the ugly. If this were a movie it would probably be rated PG 13. I could tell you the R rated version but I'll let you fill in the blanks if you want to.

In retirement I drive a limousine. Now, at the age of 64, I have no desire to be put in a position to be considered a crazy driver, though I have been one on occasion. This is, however, one crazy story. I can't help that. I don't really care if anyone believes it or not. I know these things happened. It's not a question of religious belief. It's just what I experienced. It's what I went through, without any equivocation. If all that sounds a little cynical, well just remember, I'm from Massachusetts.

Even though I live in the People's Republic of Massachusetts I consider myself a fortunate person. I have a beautiful, loving wife, and a son who is kind, intelligent and hard working. Though I am not rich, I live adequately and am able to do pretty much whatever I want to do within reason. I play in two bands and as of this writing my health is good and I am able to work in a job that I enjoy. I have been to 49 states and 15 countries and worked many years as a missionary. I once went to an unfamiliar city to work as a pioneer evangelist with nothing but a bus ticket and 10 dollars in my pocket. On the flip side, I once spent over one million dollars in less than a year. I have hung out in more fancy hotels than you can imagine. I have owned two businesses. I taught music in the public school in one of the most beautiful places on earth. I have made friends from all over the world and my Facebook network is quite large. I have lived in San Antonio, Texas where the temperature went up to 120 in the summer and spent 10 years in Pittsburg, NH where minus 45 is just another day at the beach.

I once found myself in the middle of a revolution in a city you've probably never even heard of. I once was riding on a bus through the countryside of the Soviet Union in the middle of nowhere and was pulled off the bus by plainclothes KGB agents, marched into a field with other passengers and held at gunpoint while they searched the bus for contraband.

I have also been shot at, beaten up and arrested. I have been excommunicated, abandoned by most of my friends and relatives and considered a pariah. I am a two-time cancer survivor. I have been spit on, mocked and taunted. People have robbed me and tried to kill me. Even though I am obviously white, I have sat in restaurants and been denied service as a paying customer simply because of who I was and what I represented. Employers have plotted my demise on several occasions, finding ways for me to either quit or get fired for no good reason. On the other hand, I had a boss who quit his job because he refused to go along with the higher ups and their plot to get me fired because he believed in a sense of righteousness and fair play. I was once picked up by the local sheriff, driven to the edge of town and told not to come back a la Sylvester Stallone in "Rambo." Nevertheless, even after all this and more, I consider no one as my enemy. I have no resentment or ill will towards anyone. I look back on all my experiences as lessons of life, a course given to me to create the person I was to become.

They say that a person should not toot their own horn. I have always believed that our actions should speak for themselves and that a truly humble person doesn't have to speak about themselves or what they have done. The problem is that there are a lot of people out there like me who are becoming older. Our stories may become lost forever. There are others who accomplished a lot more than I did. Some of them have passed away. There are many still living who either don't believe that they are important enough to write such a book or that they don't think they have the ability and means to do it. Perhaps they don't think that their deeds counted for much. I am just one voice. My hope is that my sharing will inspire others to share as well. Then perhaps my story will become a little more believable.

I am very happy that you are reading this book. Since you are, it may mean that you have added substantially to the quality of my life. Either that or you probably know someone who did. For those of you who have become a part of my life, whether mentioned or unmentioned, I am grateful to you. I owe you some debt. My hope is that this writing will be somewhat of a repayment of that debt. There are no bad guys here. I consider everyone mentioned in these pages as one of my family. Even if I have never met you I hope you will consider yourself also as one of my clan. We have an eternal relationship, regardless of whether you agree with these contents or not. It's OK with me if you disagree with what I did. At least you will know what happened. So then, welcome to my story.

Part of our family history towers over the City of Boston. My grandfather, William Hanlon was an electrician. In 1947 his company was commissioned to erect the light towers in Fenway Park. It's just something you might remember the next time you watch Kevin Costner and James Earl Jones driving up Massachusetts Ave. in their VW microbus in "Field of Dreams." For me though, it's something I see every day as I drive my limousine along the Massachusetts Turnpike past the Green Monster. The brilliant light of the silver structures illuminating the whole city, looking over us all, reminding me that I, like everyone, am a part of a lineage. Whatever I have done or will do in the future becomes part of the history of that lineage.

Everything you are about to read is true. I am explaining it just like it was. I am not adding anything to it or embellishing it so that you might believe something. I'm also not going to tell you that I was a perfect child who did everything perfectly in my life up until now, because I wasn't. I'm not. I'm not a guru or a prophet of some kind.

Somehow, though, I can only say that God worked in my life despite all the good and bad that I experienced. I have left the names of certain characters in this story blank. Other people have been left out entirely. If you are a part of my story and I have not included you my apologies. Please know that you are still special to me.

I have no desire to embarrass anyone or myself. Nevertheless, I have decided to include some items that had to be included so that you might understand what happened to me and to clear the air. I have written this book for church and non-church members in the hope that whoever reads it might come to understand the reality of God and the great mystery that is life from my unique perspective. Those who know me know at least some of the story. I have tried to be as forthcoming and honest as possible, and yet preserve the spirit of goodness that I experienced through all those that I have met. For any mistakes I take sole responsibility. I have come to believe, like the apostle Paul, that "All things work together for good for a man who loves the Lord." Some of these things happened long ago, but I have endeavored to preserve all the facts of the story as accurately as I can remember them.

MY PARENTS

> *Unconditional love, that they gave to me*
> *It wasn't mine to keep and I knew someday*
> *I'd hand it down to you and hope that I can be*
> *The one who makes you see*
> *The importance of unconditional love*
>   Glen Campbell from the song "Unconditional Love"

It was October 13, 1950 in Hungnam, North Korea, not one of your bucket list destinations. Here was a communist run slave labor camp where a Christian minister named Sun Myung Moon had served nearly three years. As an Allied armada of ships gathered off the coast, the bombs began to fall. The bombing destroyed the entire factory where the prisoners were working. Miraculously Rev. Moon survived the bombing. A while later surviving laborers were being summarily executed. The very next day Sun Myung Moon was due to be executed along with others in his section of the camp. Sensing the immanent invasion that very day, the prison guards vanished. Sun Myung Moon had been liberated. He headed towards Pyongyang to meet with his followers. He eventually made his way south to

Pusan with two disciples where he established the first Unification Church, a ramshackle hut made of cardboard boxes and mud. Today this movement has chapters in every country on earth with millions of members of every known race and creed.

Hungnam Fertilizer Factory and Prison Camp after
aerial bombardment in October, 1951

David Hanlon, a young seaman from Medford, Massachusetts, stood on the flight deck of the carrier U.S.S. Leyte and watched the bombing in the distance. The ship also housed hundreds of U.S. Marines who later came ashore in Hungnam. Few, if any, ever returned home. A few days after the invasion, seaman Hanlon went ashore with a friend of his on shore leave and strolled through the streets of Hungnam, believing it was safe. While the two walked together they were spotted by a lone North Korean sniper. The sniper's bullet spared young David. Unfortunately, his friend lost his life. My father, of course, never even heard of the Rev. Moon until I joined his church 26 years later.

David Hanlon married the girl of his dreams, Mary Louise McGloughlin. My mother was raised as a devout protestant. Her mother was a very active church woman in the Congregational Church of Stoneham, Massachusetts. At one point my grandmother was one of the highest ranking women in that denomination in the United States. Trained on the battlefields of France in WWI, she was a nurse her entire life, and at one point she was the oldest practicing nurse in the United States, still going right up until her passing at the age of 93. My father's parents, on the other hand, were staunch Catholics. They would constantly listen to Catholic radio broadcasts. To them, having their son marry a non-Catholic was unthinkable. They initially refused to come to the wedding. Finally, they acquiesced on the condition that all the children born would be raised Catholic. Nevertheless, growing up, I eventually felt that I was half Catholic, half protestant, a combination of both belief systems. I was their first child, born at Quonset Point Naval Air Station, Rhode Island on January 14, 1953. I have one younger brother, Steven and a sister Susan, who is the youngest.

Mom and Dad after coming home from deployment
in 1951, Stoneham Massachusetts

My father was often at sea initially. My first memory of him was a very large tattooed arm hanging over my mother's bedside one morning when he came home from a year's duty at sea. We became buddies quickly. We would ride in his 49 Ford coupe and he taught me about baseball. We played catch and I remember always having a baseball glove handy at a moment's notice. I answered to the name Roy Rogers and dressed in cowboy outfits complete with Colt 45's. Everything was good and as it should be. Our family of 3 soon became 4 and eventually 5. Fortunately, he transferred to the Air Force and for the remainder of my youth he was stateside, coming home every night for supper. As a child he was and still is my hero, despite the fact that we grew apart over the years. He did all the things that young boys aspired to be; soldier, athlete, musician and story teller. We loved to go watch him play softball at night under the lights. A third baseman, he often hit soaring home runs over the light towers. As an amateur boxer he had his nose broken many times, and having no cartilage in it, he could push it against the side of his face. Working as an airplane mechanic and turning wrenches all day for many years, no one would dream of trying to arm wrestle him.

He was a self-taught pianist, and could play hundreds of complex jazz and classical tunes by ear. He could sing funny songs or passionate love songs and could entertain any crowd with show tunes like "Wouldn't It Be Loverly" or Frank Sinatra ballads or even Debussy's "Claire de Lune."

He was, however, an agnostic. My mother was the more religious. She was church secretary at the Congregational Church of Pelham, NH for many years. Very humble and serving, she could somehow keep my father's Irish temper in check. As a military wife she had very few creature comforts that we all take for granted in today's world. Once I saw her cry because her new sewing basket was destroyed by our roughhousing. I felt so desperate to cheer her up somehow. I just wanted to comfort her in some way. I have to say that I cannot recall her ever complaining about the harsh way that the military treated the families back in those days.

My parents, like all parents, were not perfect. Once when I was a toddler they left me in a room next to an open window propped up with a piece of wood that to me looked like a toy gun. I pulled out the window stop and the window fell and broke all my fingers. Both were chain smokers, like many people of that era. Despite their faults, my parents raised me to feel that I was somehow special. Now that I am a parent myself I can see that they were, in fact, excellent. I did not feel our family was lacking in any way. It was not difficult for me to believe in God.

MY DREAM

When I was very young we lived for five years on Loring Air Force Base in Limestone, Maine, one of the coldest, most desolate places on earth. There was so much snow there that you could only tell it was spring because the snow line went down below the level of the top of the picture window in the living room. The snow became so high that shoveling was impossible so houses had doors made very high so people wouldn't get stuck coming out. There were giant snow blowers that would clear the streets by blowing the snow up over the top of the telephone wires. Streets were like canyons with snow piled right up to the level of the wires. We lived there for five years. Then one day in the dead of winter with temperatures in the minus something or other range my dad came home from work and announced the he had been transferred to Puerto Rico. Our family was to leave in two days. We boarded the plane with our winter clothing, all bundled up and arrived in San Juan at 85 degrees. All winter clothes went straight into the trash can.

We lived for a time on Ramey Air Force Base in Aguadilla, Puerto Rico, a paradise on earth if ever there was one, with beautiful beaches, warm, sunny weather with amazing wildlife and plant life. Everything seemed so different from New England. At first, we lived off base next to a sugar cane field bordering the rain forest. The beach was perhaps 3 miles away. We went there quite often, enjoying the water, my brother, Steve, and I trying to catch hermit crabs. One typical day at the beach my mother was sunning herself while the rest of us played in the sand next to her, building sand castles. We had been there for hours, when suddenly, the sand where we were playing moved and a huge sea tortoise stood up, covered up her eggs and walked slowly into the ocean. We had unknowingly been playing right on top of it for hours.

There was a tree in our front yard, which my mother labeled "The World's Ugliest Tree." It was very gnarly, had greasy leaves that did not produce any shade and had these ugly brown seed pods that hung down. My brother and I would pull the seed pods down and use them for boomerangs. Mom asked Dad to cut down the tree. Of course, not being a priority, it never got cut down and became a source of constant complaint. Then one day this miserable looking tree bloomed these brilliant red flowers the size of basketballs. These trees covered the countryside and suddenly the whole island became a dazzling crimson.....for two weeks. Then the tree, called the flamingo or flamboyant, went back to being the ugliest tree again. Needless to say, though, the tree was never cut down.

The military by 1962 was a totally integrated organization, at least for non-commissioned officers' families like ours. All races and creeds, kids came from everywhere. I made friends from all parts of the USA and from several foreign countries. I had a friend next door whose parents were Japanese. I used to go over there and eat seaweed. I liked him. He was also good at baseball. My sister at that time was about three years old.

She came home one day and said she had a boyfriend. My mom told her to invite him over for a snack. She went a few doors down and brought back this black boy, Jimmy, who was also about three. The look on my Dad's face was priceless.

Going to church was a time to talk to God. I accepted Catholicism and became an altar boy. At the age of ten I had the entire Catholic mass memorized in Latin. Sunday mass was, for me, a mystical experience. As an altar boy, I worked closely with the priests during the Sunday Service and dressed in cassock and surplus, sometimes black, sometimes red. I liked the feeling of being close to God. I didn't understand it, but it always left me with a sense of peace. I admired the sincerity of the priest, who did everything with such care and preparation. On the other hand, like most Hanlons, I got into a few fights at school. One day, Jimmy Patterson stole my marbles and I hit him in the mouth. Unfortunately, he had his mouth open and I cut my knuckle badly and had to get a tetanus shot. I still have the scar.

Mark as altar boy in 1962

My best friend, Bill Carn, was a protestant from Alabama. We did everything together; baseball every day, hanging out, riding bicycles, listening to the Beatles on 45s or LP albums. Our favorite thing to do was to take our bicycles out to the golf course and sneak out onto the fairway that was just at the edge of the runway and lay down face up, unseen in the rough. The B 52s would land and take off just feet above our heads. One day he and I walked into the NCO club on the base and put a nickel in the jukebox to listen to "I Want to Hold Your Hand" by the Beatles of course. The looks and comments we got from the soldiers there were, well, let's just say it added to my vocabulary.

One day, Bill told me he liked this girl in school. We were in the fourth grade. I sat next to this same girl in class and we were quite friendly. It didn't seem right that a girl could come between friends. Bill and I talked about girls some. We decided that Elizabeth Taylor was the most beautiful woman in the world. We were only 11 years old. What did we know? Nevertheless, it was good to have a friend that you could share everything with. It made life so much easier, the invisible bond made of trust. It was a good thing to have when the world is about to come apart under your feet.

One day I came home from school and mom said that we would not be going to school for a while. They were launching all the B 52s and sending them to Russia because the Russians were putting nuclear missiles in Cuba and pointing them at the United States. Our school became full of marines. Then we had to stay indoors for several days. It was very tense. Dad went to work and mom could not say when he was coming home. It was a very stressful week.

A few months later we heard that President Kennedy had been shot and killed. People all over the neighborhood wept. I needed to get away from this so I got on my bike and road for several miles until I came to the church that sat on a cliff overlooking the ocean. I looked out over the water and wondered what was going to happen in the future. It seemed obvious to me that there was some force at work that was trying to destroy this paradise that I wanted to keep. Soon after this we left our island paradise and came back to New England.

Around this time, I also remember having a reoccurring dream. Like many children, I had flying dreams. In my dreams I would fly anywhere. Around the house, through mountainous landscapes or even to distant planets. But there was one dream that I had that would come back every now and then. I was flying up to heaven where I would meet Jesus. I would try to enter the kingdom but he blocked my way, saying that first I had to go back down to earth and help the people to come there. I can remember having this dream at least 5 or 6 times but it may have been many more. I never told anyone about it. I thought that perhaps people would think that I was somehow strange.

Altogether I went to twelve different schools before I graduated from high school. I had to learn how to make friends quickly. It was very important to me to excel in everything. Not necessarily schoolwork mind you, but things that would help to get you friends and be popular; baseball, basketball, and of course, music. But I also liked games such as chess, spinning tops, yo-yo, pool, table tennis, table hockey, card games, card tricks, magic tricks, horseshoes, and golf. Anything that kids did together I wanted to be the best at. I loved baseball. I especially loved all the trick pitches; curve ball, fork ball, screwball, knuckle ball, epheus pitch, slider, change up, submarine pitch. I learned how to throw them all and mastered some of them as a pitcher in high school. I loved things that were a bit magical. I learned how to make a behind the back layup in basketball. I could make a layup taking the ball twice around the waist. I could throw the basketball straight up, clap ten times and catch it behind my back, not that I was any good in basketball, mind you. My athletic skills were minimal, but I loved the sport and played both baseball and basketball all through high school.

THE SEARCH FOR TRUE LOVE

> *When I was younger, so much younger than today*
> *I never needed anybody's help in any way*
> *But now those days are gone, I'm not so self assured*
> *Now I find I've changed my mind, I've opened up the doors*
> "Help" by John Lennon and Paul McCartney

ike all young boys, I wondered about love. The problem was our family had two things we would never discuss at the kitchen table; Religion and Love/Sex. Of course, these were the two things that I began to think about more and more. The older I got the more I began to realize these were the two areas that I had the most questions about and seemed to be the things that mattered most. I think this is what attracted me to Rev. Sun Myung Moon and the Unification movement more than anything. The open and honest way he discussed topics that were constantly on my mind and had been since childhood was so refreshing to me. I felt understood and validated. My parents never understood or felt capable of discussing the things that were most important to me as a teenager. I was left on my own to "figure things out" for myself. Topics of a spiritual or of

11

a sensitive nature were taboo. When I became a teenager my father and I had, "the talk." It was a 5-minute car ride, the conclusion of which I could not understand since he never said anything except that I could ask him anything anytime. It was awkward and confusing, but seemed to make him feel better at the end of the ride. Of course, it really didn't matter since I, like every teenager, already thought I knew everything. I still do. Just ask my wife, Ursula. She'll tell you.

Fortunately, I had parents who genuinely loved one another. It was obvious that they cared for and respected each other's opinions. Their actions towards each other, more than anything they said, gave me a clear idea of what I wanted in a relationship. There was never any discord within our family. I honestly cannot remember them ever arguing or fighting. Our home was a peaceful place. When I was growing up I felt that my parents were better than all other parents. But, I suppose there are a lot of people who feel the same thing. Maybe that's how we are supposed to feel about our parents. Of course, they never divorced and remained together throughout their lives.

Our family returned to New England when I was entering Junior High School, eventually settling in Pelham, NH. Our home was a beautiful white cape set back in the woods with a long driveway and a huge yard. We spent our summers at a family owned lake house on Webster Lake in Franklin, NH., one of the most beautiful places on earth in the summer. There we would swim, fish or water-ski. In the evenings we would play canasta while listening to the Red Sox on the radio. New England lakes are so calming and relaxing. The drive up to Franklin always seemed to take forever as we couldn't wait to see the lake again, smell the woodstoves and hear the sounds of the waves lapping the shore. We had our summer friends and were anxious to see them again. There was a special marker that we always looked for so we would know we were almost there, a wooden figure of Uncle Sam that greeted us when we were entering Franklin. When we saw it all of us cheered.

Dad took us out fishing almost every evening. We only went to one spot, a place determined by my grandfather on my mother's side as the best fishing spot on the lake. It was a particular unmarked spot that was at an exact right angle between the red boathouse and the second rock hazard marker. In the many years we went to that lake I fished every part of it over and over and it was true. That was the best spot. We always caught fish there. Sometimes only a few, but more often than not, each of us, my brother, sister, Dad and myself would catch four or five good keepers that we would clean and fry up the next night. Okay, okay. To be truthful, mom did most of the cleaning.

The lake house was about a block away from a train track. In the late evening a freight train from Montreal headed for Boston would come by. Its horn was audible many miles before it roared past the lake. By the time it got to our house the sound of the train was so loud it felt that it was going to come right through our bedroom. My brother Steve and I would wait up to hear the train go by. As the two of us laid in our beds we would count the numbers of cars by listening to the train wheels as they crossed the bridge. I remember that the train was sometimes over 120 cars long. One night my brother and I waited up to hear the train. He eventually fell asleep, but I still wanted to hear the train, but it never came. I listened for the faint train whistle in the distance but all I could hear was dead silence on the lake and an occasional bird or cricket. Then I remember hearing my parents whispering to each other in the next room. I could not hear anything clearly or make out any of the words, but I remember the intimate way in which they spoke to each other, with tenderness and love that I had never heard before. I realized at that moment that I was a very lucky person and that I had come from a good place. I knew from that moment that their love for each other was real. I decided right then that my purpose in life was to find what it was that my parents had. I realized that I wanted that more than anything. They were and always will be my king and queen.

I never had a steady girlfriend in junior high school or even high school for that matter. I had a way of ticking girls off somehow. I was very good at driving them away for reasons unknown to me. It's not that I didn't like them, or even one or two in particular. It's just that I didn't want to be owned or tied down in any way. Some of my friends would allow their girls to tell them how to dress or wear their hair. I didn't want to be someone's pet boyfriend. It seemed to me that was too high a price to pay for being fawned over. Besides, I was just too busy. I was a busy guy.

I played in several rock bands in junior high and high school. I loved rock music and later folk/pop. I mostly played lead guitar. I was driven by the rhythm and harmony of the music and the power expressed by 5 guys working to make one united sound. Unfortunately, every band I played in had the same problems. We would practice and get pretty good, and play a few gigs. Then the girls would come around to the rehearsals. Practicing took a back seat. Then I would yell and complain and the band would dissolve, or most likely, I would just quit. Finally, I took up folk music and went solo. I just wanted to do the music. It was frustrating.

There was one girl in junior high school who liked me for some reason. She made it known that she liked me. She came from a very poor family with many children. I felt sorry for her. She was constantly taunted by my so called friends. They tried to taunt me too but they knew I had a bit of a temper and I might extract a measure of pain on them if they pushed it too far. She was very humble and a good student. I didn't know what to make of it except that I knew that I wasn't ready for a steady in junior high. I was too busy playing basketball, baseball and rock music. I also played the clarinet and was taking private lessons. At our 25th high school reunion I met her and her husband. Her last name was now Leer. You got it. That Leer, the one that builds the sleek corporate jets. They came to the reunion in one of them. It was sweet revenge for her I am sure, and I was happy for her.

There were several boys in junior high who did have steady girlfriends, of course. Later, in high school, it became more difficult because there was so much pressure to date and go steady. It seemed that everyone was paired off. That is everyone, it seemed, except me. Even my best friend, Bruce, had a very serious girlfriend all through high school. When we went anywhere by car I was either driving or sitting in the back seat by myself. It seemed that any girl I became friendly with quickly moved on. One even got married to her older stepbrother. Another one decided she was really a lesbian after all. By the time high school ended everything seemed pretty bleak on the relationship front. However, I was learning some valuable lessons.

Looking back, it's obvious that someone was looking out for me, though at the time I thought that I was somehow cursed. One Saturday afternoon my father loaned me his brand new Buick Electra 226. This car was really fancy with a huge back seat, electric everything, sound system and a powerful V8 engine. He told me I could go over to my friend's house and nowhere else. I drove over to my friend Bruce's house and pulled the big turquoise blue four door sedan into the driveway. He had a couple of girls there already. They were a couple of his "groupies". That is, they were younger and impressionable. One of them saw the car and said, "Let's go for a ride." I should have seen the sign right there that said, "trouble ahead." We rode for a while and someone asked me how fast the car would go. We were on a straight away going through an apple orchard so I said "okay, let's see." I punched it and quickly got it up to about 95. I saw the red stop sign about a quarter mile ahead.

However, when I attempted to put on the brakes the pedal went all the way to the floor. There were no brakes, at all. The car gradually slowed down but I went through the stop sign doing at least 45. There was nowhere to go except up the driveway of this house. There were children playing in the yard, dad mowing the grass. I scooted alongside of the garage and into the back yard, took down the clothesline and dodged some white pines before the car came to rest in a pile of pine needles. The girls pounded on me and ran away. Bruce and I pushed the brand new Buick Electra out onto the street. Unbelievably there was not a scratch on it. I called my dad and just told him the brakes went out. The car had picked up a "y" shaped branch that pinched a tiny six inch piece of rubber brake line, causing the brakes to fail. I told the whole story to my dad years later. The family got a good laugh over it but I was happy that I had finally told him the whole story, embarrassing as it was.

Of course, I was curious about what it was that all these high school couples were experiencing. Some boys told everything about their conquests though I suspect some of them were outright lying to make themselves look like mighty conquerors of the opposite sex. This painted a very confusing picture in my head of what love is. By now I was a senior in high school. At that point it was very easy to forget my idealism and just allow myself to experience what all my friends were bragging about.

I had a job after school some days and on weekends at the local golf course, working as a groundskeeper. On those days I would take a different school bus and just go straight to work after school. There was one particular girl who regularly rode that bus. She and I were members of the school band. Sometimes we would go on band trips for events to different towns. There was a gay oboe player who always tried to sit next to me on the band bus. I would ask her to sit next to me on the trips so this guy wouldn't get the wrong idea. I wanted to take away any chance that he would sit next to me as he was very persistent and touchy-feely. I never said two words to this girl other than when on the occasional bus trip. It did seem, however, that she was becoming a little too friendly over time.

One day we got off the bus and I headed down the road towards the golf course. Her house was in the other direction but as we walked together she said with a big smile that she was going to take a short cut through the woods at the golf course. Well to make a long story short there were soon clothes flying this way and that. All during this though I began to feel very uncomfortable. I was not ready for this. I knew that I was not in love with this girl. It wasn't right. I couldn't go through with it.

I apologized and left. I was a couple of minutes late for work but I was still intact. I breathed many sighs of relief. It felt good somehow knowing that I was doing the right thing. I kicked myself for allowing myself to get that close to disaster. I decided that if I was going to get in that position again it was going to be under my terms and with the person that I loved and cared for deeply. That's how my high school career ended. College, well, that was a different matter.

U MASS LOWELL

> *I'm just the man in the middle*
> *Of a complicated plan.*
> *No one to show me the signs.*
> *I'm just a creature of habit*
> *In a complicated world.*
> *Nowhere to run to.*
> *Nowhere to hide, to hide, to hide, to hide....*
>
> "Man in the Middle", by The Bee Gees

B y the time I entered college life the world was in disarray. It was 1971 and the Vietnam War was raging; race riots, Kent State. Most of my friends considered themselves hippies though by now we had gone our separate ways. I dressed in traditional hippie garb; headband, bell bottom blue jeans, tank top, army jacket and motorcycle boots. My hair was the style of Jim Morrison and I had a mustache and long Elvis style sideburns. I lived at home and commuted to Lowell Tech where I was expected to study engineering. It was a miserable educational experience with long, boring lectures in classes of 300 and impossibly long and tedious homework assignments. It seemed to me that the school was training students to lob explosive projectiles on people. There was not a single class that I enjoyed. I had no friends and didn't really want any. My grades were less than mediocre. The second semester was even worse. I had to live in this miserable dormitory. My roommate never took a bath, did laundry, or changed his bed linens and listened to Aerosmith music all night long. I felt like I was a dead man slowly going insane.

Like many college students I made some bad lifestyle choices. I also had a girlfriend from home that I saw on weekends, but I treated her quite badly. Eventually, we went our separate ways. I hung out for several months with a pretty dark crowd. One of my associates was later killed in a drug deal and another I recently found out is still serving a 66 year sentence in Walpole Penitentiary for child abuse, a habit he picked up a few years after I decided to split the Pelham, NH scene. I consumed somewhat large portions of alcohol on occasions. My earlier idealistic self was at one point nearly extinguished. One thing began to happen though. I began to think about God, the purpose of life, and about what kind of person I really wanted to be. I remember one day looking in the mirror and thinking how much I really did not like the kind of person I had become. I really couldn't recognize the person looking back at me. I thought about my family and all the wonderful things I had experienced as a child. I decided to change. I cut my hair and decided to dress more normally. My former associates got left in the dust. I also realized that I needed to do something that I liked to do in order to reclaim my former self. I changed majors and decided to study music.

Studying music was a totally different experience. I was accepted at Lowell State College (which later became UMass Lowell) as a clarinet player after practicing like a dog all summer. I also played guitar here and there. Every day was fun, interesting and rewarding. I started making friends at school. Time flew by and my spirit brightened considerably. I occasionally hung out with friends from home but most of my time was spent at school, practicing four to six hours per day, studying and hanging around with other music students at the pool table in the rec room. I even got invited to a few parties, but I never felt comfortable at parties and they tended to depress me. Nevertheless, I did go to a couple of them.

I know that if I say that I met someone at UMass Lowell and eventually got married this is going to shock a lot of people who are near and dear to me, but I only relay this part of the story because; one, it is the truth and two, it is a necessary aspect of understanding who I am today. My relatives and friends from high school and college know this part of the story all too well. It was, as you will later see, part of God's plan for me. Her name was Jeanne.

Around this time, I found a new best friend in college, Ray Melanson, originally an art student from Canada. He and his wife Marilyn were devout Christians. Marilyn was an amazing violinist. She was first chair in the Lowell State Symphony Orchestra. Before they married, Ray said he was going to win her heart by learning the violin. I thought he was joking. Violin is not something you can just pick up on a whim because you want to impress some chick. Nevertheless, he practiced day and night. Listening to him practice was very painful, but he improved steadily and was accepted into the music program. By the time I graduated he was first chair and she was second chair. Both Jeanne and I and the Melansons played in the orchestra. I was the bass clarinet player and later became the first chair clarinet. By the time I was a senior I was the top clarinet player in the music department that had 40 clarinet majors. I loved the orchestral music, especially the classics like Beethoven, Brahms, Mahler and Tchaikovsky. The music seemed to take me to another plane and elicited deep emotions that were so refreshing to me spiritually and even physically.

Ray and Marilyn seemed to have an excellent relationship. They witnessed to us now and then. Jesus was a big part of their life. I began to think more about religion and God. I struggled with some of the doctrinal approach to the Bible and had some basic questions about the purpose of life. I decided I needed a showdown prayer with God. One afternoon while I was sitting in the bathtub (We had no shower), I asked God a simple prayer and that is, "Who am I in all of this plan? Please show me a picture of who I am and how I am to understand our relationship." As I looked at the end of the tub, I saw this.

To me this translated as;

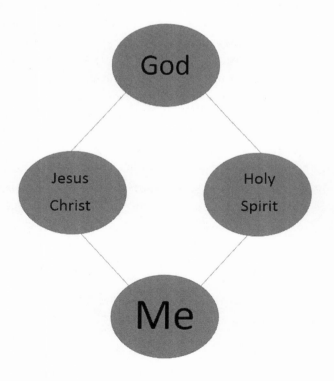

This four-position foundation made sense to me. It was like a light went on in my head. I was being reborn through the love of God by Jesus and the Holy spirit as a child of God. Later when I heard the Divine Principle (specifically the chapter entitled Christology) I understood my "revelation" and what it meant. I would also come to understand the meaning of Gen 1:28 (be fruitful, multiply and have dominion) and the Three Great Blessings.

I was starting to read the Bible and became a genuine born again Christian. I became a member of the Immanuel Baptist Church of Chelmsford Massachusetts. Jeanne and I both got baptized. I taught Sunday School and played some music at the church from time to time. She and I even had our senior recital there. I still had some questions that I wanted answers for, but basically my spiritual life was becoming an active one. I wasn't a doctrinal fundamentalist per se, but I liked the security of being amongst people who seemed sure of their beliefs, despite what their detractors said. I found that most people who hated the Christian students like us were living lifestyles that I had already decided against.

The Melansons and the Hanlons hung out together a lot. We did more than just go to church events. We went up to Canada on vacation and visited Ray's relatives. We climbed Mt. Katahdin and walked across the Knife's Edge. We did go to some church seminars and witnessed to people door to door. I even got one young man to join that church. A year later, when I was already a member of the controversial Unification Church, this young man came to me to tell me about what the Bible "really meant." It was, however, impossible to explain to him what I had learned.

After graduation in 1976 the Hanlons and the Melansons decided to move out of Lowell and find an apartment where we could share expenses, perhaps out in the country a ways in a more decent area. The day we looked for a new place we got together and prayed, "Heavenly Father, please guide us to a place according to your will." The place we found was half of a large old farm house on a country road in Hollis, New Hampshire (population in 1976, maybe 500). Unbeknownst to us, this house was less than a mile down the road from another house used as a church witnessing center, by the Holy Spirit Association for the Unification of World Christianity, a.k.a. the Unification Church.

HOLLIS, NH

> *Sail on home to Jesus won't you good girls and boys*
> *I'm all in pieces, you can have your own choice*
> *But I can hear a heavenly band full of angels*
> *And they're coming to set me free*
>
> *I don't know nothing 'bout the why or when*
> *But I can tell that it's bound to be*
> *Because I could feel it, child, yeah*
> *On a country road*
>
> James Taylor, "Country Road"

n November of 1976 I was working in a music store in Nashua New Hampshire where I gave lessons and occasionally worked in the sales department. I had 40 private students and played a few gigs here and there. The owner of the store gave me a new job to open a temporary store for the Christmas season in a little mall in Salem, New Hampshire. It was not much more than a booth but it had a lot of foot traffic and there were 50 or 60 other small stores and restaurants in the building. November, as you can imagine, was quite slow. There was a lot of time to chat with the other store employees.

As it so happened, the store right next to mine was a small booth that sold ginseng tea, marble vases and butterflies mounted in jars. The people who operated the booth were quite friendly. They had several employees but the booth was only operated by one person at a time. I got to know some of them and found out that they were all a part of a religious community in Hollis of all places, and that their house was just down the road from ours. They came from all over, none from New Hampshire, and all lived at the house in Hollis. Some of them were from Japan and Europe. Hollis to Salem is quite a ride, 30 to 40 minutes, so we decided we would share rides when appropriate.

It seemed that all the employees would read the same book, a black book that would sit on their desk day after day. Each member seemed to have one. One day one of the employees asked me if I would watch her booth as she went to the restroom. I opened the book and just scanned its contents. The first page I opened to was a picture of an oriental man in a toga. The second page I opened to spoke of the I Ching, Yin Yan, and other oriental concepts. I closed the book and thought to myself, "Wow, it's an oriental cult." There was one girl, Cathy, from Colorado who would ride home with me quite often. She was a little pushy but she was cute and very friendly. We had these theological discussions every night on the way home for 30 to 40 minutes. She asked me all kinds of questions like, "What do you think of John the Baptist?" and "Is there life after death?" or "What was the fall of man?" These were questions that I had been seeking answers to. My studies had only come up with partial answers to them. I would tell her what I thought and she would say, "Well, that's a traditional understanding," or something to that effect. I would say something like "That's the only understanding." Her responses were somewhat unnerving but tweaked my curiosity. Then she would invite me over to hear a lecture. This happened several times but each time I declined. Then one evening she said, "and dinner" and I thought "Ok, I'll come for dinner."

A few days later Jeanne and I went over to the center for dinner. It was a very warm atmosphere with excellent food that I had never eaten before; Korean and Japanese laid out so nicely. There were perhaps seven members there and the two of us. It was really a treat. I played them a few songs on the guitar that they had lying around and we heard a lecture. The lecture didn't really speak to me but we had a good time. Jeanne was happy that she had made some new friends.

We went over a few more times after that. One time they showed us a video (back then it was 16 millimeter film) of a speech given by Rev. Sun Myung Moon at Madison Square Garden. When I first saw him, I remember commenting that he looked somewhat like my Dad. Back in those days they really did look alike; short, round face, heavy set but muscular, weathered complexion, powerfully built with short thick fingers. I am sure my comment surprised them all. In the Unification Church, Rev. Moon is referred to as Father Moon or True Father.

After the Christmas season the mall closed and I didn't see much of the Unification people. I also had two jobs at this point. I was still working at the music store but I also went back to work at the golf course. I was becoming a workaholic. Jeanne, however, had more free time and went over to the center occasionally. By now they were asking us if we would go to a weekend workshop. Sometimes they would come over to our house to pick up Jeanne. They always asked me to come as well but I would come up with some excuse not to go.

One Saturday morning my wife told me that we were invited for the afternoon over to the center and suggested that I come along as well. It just so happened that day I had a good excuse. My car had a broken windshield wiper motor. It had not worked at all for more than a week. Saturday was the only day I had to replace it. Back then I was a pretty good mechanic and loved to tinker with cars. I could pretty much take a car apart and put it back together. Ernest Planck, the center director and a few members came by for Jeanne. They tried to get me to come along as well. I explained about the car but they were not deterred so I decided to demonstrate the problem. I turned the wiper switch and, lo and behold, it worked perfectly. Now I had to go over to the center. Admittedly we did have a good time. I also got recruited to become the church mechanic and went over there from time to time to help them with their vehicles. I would do tune ups, oil changes and minor repair jobs for them. By the way, the windshield wiper motor never worked again and I did have to replace it; another coincidence, perhaps.

Around this time, I had heard a few negative comments from my brother and sister when I mentioned who Jeanne and I had been hanging out with. My brother told me that a few students from the University of New Hampshire, where he was attending, had disappeared from school and joined the group from one day to the next, just abandoning their studies suddenly. My sister also became quite alarmed. She had heard a few things as well. It also seemed that the church was involved in a court case with the State of New Hampshire involving illegal fundraising. I, however, had no intention of joining this group of single people anyways, though it seemed to me that they could not be talking about the same group.

Then, one Friday in late March, I came home from work and Jeanne said "Mark, I have signed us up for the weekend workshop." Tired and not in the mood I replied, "No, let's just call them back and cancel." Her reply was "No, Mark, I signed up for the weekend workshop and I've already paid for both of us." It seemed the decision was already made for me. I pondered just calling them to ask for our money back, but decided that would not be good form. I somewhat reluctantly decided to go. A few hours later we were picked up at our house and off we went to Marblehead, Massachusetts. During the ride I felt a little better about making the decision to go. I did genuinely like the people. I also realized that I should be there if for no other reason than to make sure that Jeanne didn't get carried away and actually join this group. It was now the 3rd week of March, 1977.

THE WORKSHOP

The Lord into his garden comes
The spices yield a rich perfume
The lilies grow and thrive
The lilies grow and thrive

Refreshing showers of grace divine
From the Father flow to every vine
And make the dead revive
And make the dead revive

Song of the Garden (Appalachian melody)

I was genuinely surprised to see the workshop place. It was a magnificent mansion that sat on a cliff overlooking the ocean. It had a wraparound porch facing the bay and standing on it looking out into the sea you could hear the constant sound of waves crashing onto the beach and the cry of seagulls swirling overhead and perched on rocks. It was the most beautiful house I had ever seen. There were about 40 people at the workshop, 10 or so were new guests like myself. Some had just joined in the last few weeks or months and some had been members for 2 or three years. Many of them were part of a traveling team of missionaries that kept moving from state to state.

Before every lecture there were a few songs, some spiritual, others were common folk and pop melodies that had a bit of a message. I enjoyed singing the songs and learning some of the new ones. The song leaders were not professional but very sincere and good hearted. Everyone seemed "nice." There were no abrasive personalities except for mine perhaps. I listened to the lectures intently, but sat in the back with the back of the chair leaning against the wall. I was determined not to let anyone think that I was having a good time.

We had group discussions that gave everyone a chance to share about themselves and what they were experiencing. I liked some of the guests but I really enjoyed the company of the members, especially the ones who had been around for a while. There was one tall Texan, David Cantrell, who had a funny sense of humor. He and I became friends and remain so even to this day. I ran into him not so long ago at the 40th anniversary of Rev. Moon's Yankee Stadium Speech. It had been many years since we last spoke. We reminisced about meeting at Marblehead way back in 77. His accent is so thick. The sound of his voice is still one of the friendliest God ever created.

At the workshop I asked him and a few others all the questions I could think of. I also found that the lectures themselves were in fact answering a lot of the questions that would pop into my mind, even before asking them. By now I was not sitting in the back. I started to take notes.

The songs also had quite an effect on me, especially the Unification Church songs, known as Holy Songs. The words were so deep and soulful. They were very unique and created a very peaceful and serene atmosphere. Some of the rousing numbers really cleared the air and were very animated and energetic, but not in a contrived way. There were perhaps 20 or so people singing in the lectures, but as we sang I could swear that it sounded like the voices of many times more.

They say that the eyes are the window to the soul. Unificationist detractors also say never to look Unificationists in the eyes or you will be "brainwashed." I played baseball in high school. Back in the day I was a pretty good pitcher. When I pitched I tried to look the batters in the eye. I could see their fear and intimidate them with a look. On the other hand, some batters would try to stare me down. During the workshop I tried to get a sense of where people were at. The song leaders, Linda Corrigan and

Tom Carter, especially impressed me. During the songs, when I looked them in the eye I felt genuineness coming from them. Often teary eyed with joy coming from their hearts, their demeanor was totally sincere. I could not believe that there were people like this. I realized that I had become somewhat jaded and felt very grateful to be there.

I listened to the prayers of some of the members. Their prayers were so moving and sincere. Sometimes they would shed tears while praying as did others while listening. I was not a stranger to prayer, but this was far beyond what I had experienced in church. I became quite jealous of these members who could speak so intimately with God. Their love for God seemed so real in prayer. Sometimes when we prayed on the beach we held hands and I could feel the energy of the prayer in the circle when I closed my eyes. When we prayed individually at night spread out along the waterfront I felt a comforting warmth and a sense of wellbeing that I had never felt before.

I began to realize that The Divine Principle was not an ordinary teaching. Its compelling logic and depth are transforming. This is the conclusion I came to before we were even half way through the lectures. It was having an illuminating effect on me and most of the guests as well. To me the teaching was electrifying and perfect. Even though it is logical and systematic, it is a vast teaching covering many areas. The conclusion of the Divine Principle as taught in the three days workshop has to do with the Second Advent of Christ, specifically how, when and where he shall return. All of the topics, including Christology, Predestination and all of the others, were discussed thoroughly and fairly. I could not find any flaw in it. I have been searching for one now for 40 years. To this day I have not found anyone who can argue successfully with its precepts, either in general or in detail. To me, it is simply the truth. The more I have studied, the more truth I find in it.

I know what you're thinking. Food deprived, sleep deprived, this boy is being led down the primrose path. Honestly, there was way too much food. Besides, have you seen me lately? Also, there was a curfew that was strictly observed. It was an intense 3 days yes, but we did sports (volleyball) and played games on the beach in the afternoon. These were welcome breaks from the intensity of the lectures. By that I don't mean to infer that the lectures or the lecturers were overbearing, because they were not. It's just that the content was very new and thought provoking. I realized that I could not memorize everything but I wrote down questions and thoughts that came into my head so that later I could fill in the blanks.

Finally, at the end of the 3 day workshop, we were given an opportunity to stay and study for another week. At this point I had not thought about joining. I discussed this with Jeanne and we decided that we would like to stay another 7 days and review the teachings in further depth before making any commitment to do anything. I made arrangements at work to have the week off.

The lecturer at the three day workshop was Richard Jones. His lectures were very meticulous. He is a graphic artist, so all his diagrams were perfect, using multicolored chalk and he filled up blackboard after blackboard of perfectly arranged, systematic diagrams and numbered outline main points, which he explained sequentially. He really is a great lecturer. I have tried to duplicate his style of lecture, but my left handed, barely legible scrawl is pitiful in comparison. Nevertheless, I have become a pretty good lecturer, according to some.

The seven days lecturer was Henri Schauffler. His lectures were quite different. He took more time with each topic, but he is a very passionate speaker. His lectures were longer and had much more detail, but had an emotional appeal that I found compelling. He was also older and the only married person in the workshop. When he spoke of God's heart or Jesus' suffering I could not help but feel something inside myself that identified with this unique view of the Bible, history, and the purpose of life. Nothing could have made more sense. Never in my life did I dream that I would hear something so profound. I felt chills, tears of joy, and an incredible warm sense of wellbeing as the 7 days flew by.

It wasn't just the lectures that sold me on Unificationism. I wanted to know if the members themselves believed all of this and what their commitment was. I wanted to know if it was just me that was experiencing this. I also needed to ask God whether this was true or not. To me, nothing short of a direct answer from him was going to be enough for me to make the kind of lifestyle changes that the others had obviously made. After all the lectures we heard a talk about the history of the Unification Movement and its founder, Rev. Sun Myung Moon. It didn't take a rocket scientist to figure out what they were saying. Hearing the conclusion meant you really couldn't sit on the fence. I never thought of myself as someone who would run away from difficulties when they arise, but this? I never expected to have something like this laid in my lap. To accept the teaching meant that you had to deal with the conclusion as well. What was I supposed to do? Why me?

THE RING

The moment of truth finally came at the end of the seven days workshop. By the last day I still had not decided what I was going to do. I was also concerned about Jeanne. She was having a good time but I sensed from her that she was assuming that we were just going to go home later that evening. I became very sullen. I knew that to be a Unificationist meant that we were to fulfill the three Great Blessings, but to receive the marriage blessing there was a period of separation necessary for everyone, including married couples. That's why it was easier back then for single people to join. Unificationist marriages meant that we were reclaiming our position as restored Adam and Eve, prior to the fall. That meant we had to live a platonic relationship conditionally for an unknown period, and back in 1977 that was perhaps as long as 3½ years (Nowadays the standard period of separation for married couples is 40 days). That's quite a step to make suddenly. I wasn't sure I could make that step. I also wasn't sure if my wife, Jeanne, whom I did love and wanted to keep would be willing to do this.

I was beside myself with anxiety. Either I was going to go home and be a "B" type member or I was going to jump into this thing with both feet as a full-time member. I couldn't imagine just going home and trying to live a normal life after what I had just heard. I also wanted to be a part of this new movement and take this journey with these new friends I had just met. I wanted to be a part of the building of the Kingdom of Heaven on the earth. I still do, even now, in 2017. I also knew that, to others, doing that would seem really irresponsible and would be impossible to explain easily to my friends and relatives. I wanted to do the most responsible thing, but I wasn't sure yet what that was.

The last thing before the workshop officially ended was a volleyball game at a park in Marblehead. There was a pond near the volleyball court. Of course, there was no way I could play volleyball at that moment. I needed time to think, so I walked down to the edge of the pond and stared into the depths. Gazing into the water, searching for an answer in the waves and sparkles of shimmering light, I asked God to please tell me what to do. It was the sincerest prayer I ever prayed.

Just at that moment the volleyball from the game came bounding down the hill and went into the water. As a strong gust of wind was blowing the ball out into the middle of the pond some of the players yelled "Get the ball!" I was the only one who could retrieve it before it went out of reach. I thought to myself, "Ok, I'll jump in if you want me to." At that moment I also thought to myself that this might be a way to snap out of my funk, a step of faith so to speak. I waded out into the icy cold water until it was nearly over my head and grabbed the ball just before the wind took it away. I grabbed the ball with my left hand, took a few steps towards the shore, and being left handed, threw it with that same hand. As I did that my wedding ring, which had never been removed from my finger since October 11th, 1975, flew off and disappeared into that lake forever. It was like a force pulled it off me. I can still see the shining gold band spinning round and round and falling into the dark water. It's like a video clip that plays over and over in my head. I sat down on the shore. I could barely breathe. People asked me if I was alright.

31

That seemed like a clear enough sign for me. I cried many tears for an hour or so. I decided to trust God with my life from that moment. I told Jeanne of my decision. We decided to join the church and work as full-time missionaries.

THE ADVENTURE BEGINS

> *No more will I down primrose paths wander, as in days gone by;*
> *But the track of the white trefoil I will follow, till the day I die.*
> *Though the serpent tries to effect disguise,*
> *At my three questions he'll quiver and cower,*
> *As he's reminded once again that he's very near the end,*
> *When he'll be blinded by the morning's dawning hour.*
>
> "The Perfect Child" by Chris Davies

We cleared out our things from our apartment much to the shock of our good friends Ray and Marilyn. They thought we were crazy. I was reluctant to try to explain too much but I am sure they felt insulted and betrayed in a way. They came over to the center to try to dissuade us from joining once and we went over the basic Divine Principle with them, but they saw this as way too drastic a step. Nevertheless, I was convinced that I was in fact doing the right thing.

Starting this adventure, my thought was that at some point Jeanne and I would receive the Blessing of Marriage and that we had nothing to be concerned about as long as we continued this course. It was suggested that we should perhaps work in separate locations as it would make it easier to focus and that we would meet or phone from time to time or visit our relatives, etc. This sounded like a good plan so I worked in Hollis and my wife worked in Boston at the church center at 46 Beacon St.

At first everything worked according to plan. I enjoyed being a full time missionary in the center. I would study Divine Principle, the Bible, and Rev Moon's speeches and do some witnessing in Nashua. I had already witnessed some as a Baptist, so that activity was not new to me. We found some guests and witnessed to one Lutheran pastor. I tried my hand at a little fundraising, something that was entirely new to me. Going shop to shop or door to door and soliciting funds by offering items like butterflies in jars was very much out of my comfort zone, though I understood the need for this activity. I gradually got somewhat used to it, especially since we were also witnessing at the same time. Occasionally we would meet some resistance from some people or a few harsh negative comments, but generally I felt getting out and meeting people on the street was in a way good for me as it expanded my ability to relate to all types of people. We fundraised in all kinds of neighborhoods; white, black, Hispanic, Jewish, Portuguese, you name it. I took one trip up the coast of Maine with my friend David Cantrell, who was the Maine state director. We went all the way up to the Canada border selling butterflies in jars, going shop to shop. The scenery was spectacular and we completely sold out of everything. We made about 1,000 dollars in 2 days which to me was an incredible sum, especially since I had been applying for teaching jobs that were offering 7,000 dollars per year, and those jobs were impossible to get because most of them had over 100 applicants.

Life in the center did become more and more difficult, though. I was a very ambitious, gung ho young member. I realized that some of the members did struggle with things and personalities tended to grate on one another over time. I learned a little about how hard restoration is, a big theme in Divine Principle. One time I got into this stupid argument with the center director, Ernie, about how to make Easter eggs. I was sure he was wrong and I was right. I was also quite exhausted. At some point I had had it. This Kingdom of Heaven stuff was just a pipedream, a crock of

I decided to leave and announced that I was going to Boston to pick up my wife and that was it. I was halfway out the door, steam coming out of the top of my head. My Irish blood was boiling. Catherine, the young sister from Colorado, approached me and got me to calm down. Her soothing voice made me see reason. I realized how easy it was for Cain to kill Abel. I had never been so angry in my life. Why? Over a stupid Easter egg.

In retrospect, I wondered where all these emotions had come from. In my mind, I knew the answer. I apologized to Ernie, who had showed me such care and concern for all the time I had been there. From that moment on, I felt like a real member. I knew that we were fighting a battle against a powerful and devious enemy, one who is determined to keep us from appreciating the value of others as well as our own value, one who would do anything to prevent us from achieving the goal of accomplishing the Three Great Blessings.

That night I went to bed feeling good, but beyond exhausted. I fell asleep in the bedroom in my sleeping bag on the floor, which is how we slept back in those days. I estimate that I slept a total of ten years on the floor. I still can do it when I have to. Nowadays camping in the woods on a floor of pine needles feels soft in comparison to those days, yet I have to say that sleeping on floors was more restful in a way than in any bed.

Anyways, that evening I woke up in the middle of the night having to use the bathroom. There were several other guys sleeping on the floor and I didn't want to wake them so I made my way to the hallway without my slippers, which I always wore. I could not find them in the dark. To me there were only two things in life that I needed to have absolutely wherever I went. One was a fingernail/toenail clipper and the other a good pair of slippers. If I went on a trip and didn't have both of those items I would become very negative. Anything else I could do without, except maybe a baseball hat.

I went to the restroom, washed my face and hands, dried off with a towel, came out and opened the door to the bedroom. I could see into the room because of the light from the hallway. There were several sleeping bags scattered about the room, but there in the middle of the room was an old man standing in my slippers. Not any old man, mind you, but my grandfather from my mother's side who had passed away a month or two before I was born. He walked around the room slowly and back to his original spot, looked over at me and disappeared, leaving the slippers as they were.

It felt very natural to see him, the message he wanted to convey to me obvious and done without words. In my life I have had a handful of experiences such as this. They are a part of my life, but by no means a major part. I do not think they are necessary or at times desirable. Nevertheless, I have found that God occasionally gives them to me when he wants to get my attention or say something. I don't go looking for them or expect them as some other people might. They are gifts after all and I think they should be treated as such. Nevertheless, this was the first time I had experienced anything remotely like this. It was totally unexpected and out of the blue.

Before I joined the church I did have one experience, however, that made me think about the paranormal and that there is more to our existence than what we can experience with our five senses. When I was a teenager we lived in Pelham, NH at 3 Livingston Rd., in a beautiful white cape set back from the road with a long driveway through white pines and grassy front yard. When we first moved in the house was new. It had a sand point well in the back yard that supplied water. A sand point well is a cheap well, basically a pipe in the ground. Eventually this well dried up and we had no water. My father had two choices for a solution. One was to drill an artesian well which is a very deep well drilled through layers of rock. This option was the preferred option but cost several thousand dollars, money that our family did not have. The other option was to call a diviner, someone who can sense where water is under the ground with no equipment other than a branch from a tree. The diviner would find the water and a backhoe would come, dig a large hole and then cement tiles would be placed in the bottom of the hole. My father had no faith that this option would work, but it cost 20 bucks for the diviner and another 200 for the backhoe so he decided to give it a try.

The diviner came over and proceeded to cut down a "y" shaped branch from one of the white pines in our yard. I watched him pace about the yard holding the two handles of the stick with the end pointing horizontally forward. As he continued to walk occasionally the stick would go down in 3 or 4 places as if pulled down. Watching this, I thought to myself that this is phony baloney. My dad and I looked at each other with skeptical "yeah right" looks. When the diviner was about finished he asked me if I would hold one end of the stick. He and I walked across the front yard together. When we got to a certain point the stick pulled down. "A yup. This is the place alright. Mr. Hanlon, if you dig right heeyah you'll find the watta is 18 feet down. Ya see there's a vein going thisa way that intersects with anotha one running off yonda. If you dig hea you'll find watta at 18 feet and it'll pump at 6 gallons a minute." I thought to myself again "Yeah, right."

Soon the backhoe drove in the yard and proceeded to dig a huge hole as we watched. Ten feet, nothing. Fifteen feet, nothing but sand. Eighteen feet, still nothing and my dad started to turn red. The backhoe could only dig to twenty feet without expanding the hole greatly. At twenty feet there was still nothing and my dad got on the phone with the diviner. At this point I was glad I was not that guy, still the diviner insisted that there was water there. Now the backhoe driver became a little miffed so he decided to climb down into the hole. I watched as they lowered the extension ladder down into this deep hole. The backhoe driver climbed down the ladder and jumped off at the bottom into the center of the hole where he went waist deep in mud. The water was there all along as some floating particles of sand on the water had hidden its presence. The tiles were installed and to this day, now fifty years later, the water level is a consistent 18 feet and pumps year round at 6 gallons per minute, a fact verified recently by the present owner, Jeff Hassan.

Dug well, water discovered by diviner in 1966

This event stuck with me. I came to have a kind of reverence for that well. When I drive by there occasionally I can't help but recall this incident with a sense of awe.

On April 18th all of us loaded up into my Ford Econoline van, which I eventually donated to the church, and headed to the Manhattan Center in New York to hear Rev. Moon speak at a church holiday called Parents

Day. Back then there were only the four major holidays; God's Day, Parents Day, Children's Day and The Day of All Things. These holidays signified key providential accomplishments in the ministry of Rev. Moon and the Unification Church.

I estimate that there were perhaps 3000 people in this large hall on 34th street and 8th Ave. I sat about 20 rows back so I had a good view. This was the first of many such events that I attended in this building. A few months ago I took my family to NY to hear Mrs. Moon give a speech and remember sitting in exactly the same spot way back in 1977. Now the building is a fantastic high tech performance theater with state of the art video and sound recording, but it cannot rival the excitement and anticipation of those days, hearing the voice of Father Moon for the first time.

It was hard to follow the details of the speech as he spoke in Korean with English translation. I was not accustomed to listening to someone speak for 4 or 5 hours and a lot of what he said went by me, but one thing is for sure. There has never been, nor will there ever be a public speaker with as much passion, emotion and endurance as Rev. Sun Myung Moon. The man is simply astounding. Having studied many of his speeches and attended over 100 of them over the years, I never attended one that he didn't give his full energy and time. His speeches were never less than 3 hours and more often went 8. I once heard him speak for 22 hours with stops only for dinner and bathroom.

After the speech there was evening entertainment from very talented members including a full chorus called the New Hope Singers International, a rock band called Sunburst and a fantastic dance team called the Little Angels of Korea. At the end of the concert some of Rev. Moon's children sang, then Rev. Moon sang with his wife and by himself. It was the perfect ending to a perfect day. Over the years many older members, such as myself, saw many such gatherings. Most of us long for those days that have long since passed.

Life in the center continued smoothly for a month or so after I joined. I was becoming accustomed to this new lifestyle; spartan to be sure, yet each day was purposeful and full of new adventures. Jeanne lived in the Boston Church where she worked as a cook and occasionally fundraised and witnessed. In June things suddenly changed, as they often do in the Unification Church.

MFT

Let me tell you about MFT. The words mean "Mobile Fundraising Team." Basically, MFT is a team of missionaries that travels throughout the country raising funds for the activities of the church. It is also a basic activity, meant not only to raise funds for church purposes, but to develop character and restore the creation. I won't dwell on the theology of MFT, but it is a very challenging and difficult lifestyle, testing the limits of physical and spiritual endurance. It's not a life for the faint of heart. It can be dangerous at times. It is a totally sacrificial lifestyle.

By the time I joined the National MFT in late June of 1977 there were several thousand young people doing this activity throughout the country. I volunteered to join MFT because of the challenge that it presented. I saw it as a shortcut to where I wanted to go on my spiritual journey. To be honest though, I was fascinated with the idea of traveling throughout the United States, though my time on MFT only took me as far as New Jersey and New York State.

As I prepared to leave for MFT I couldn't help but think that this is really going to be a big step for me. I was leaving the comfort of my hometown for the first time in my life. Some of the center members had already been on MFT. The testimonies I got from them were giving me mixed feelings. They told me a few of their stories and though they tried to encourage me, I got the feeling that this was not going to be as easy as it first seemed to be. It wasn't. Nevertheless, as I look back upon those days I feel a sense of pride and accomplishment. I felt as though I were a soldier going off to war. In reality that's exactly what it was, and in some ways it was certainly much harder. I stood at the bus station waiting for the bus to take me to NY. I carried with me everything I owned in the world: A duffle bag full of clothing, towels and toiletries, a suit bag with a couple of white shirts, dress pants and ties, a sleeping bag and a briefcase that contained a Divine Principle Book, a Bible, a couple of speeches and some writing materials and stamps. The briefcase was a going away present from Ernie and the center members.

After a brief meeting in New York with about 50 or so new MFT volunteers, myself and a few others who had been assigned to the New Jersey MFT were picked up by van and headed to Piscataway, New Jersey, which would be my home for the next few months. As I entered the suburban house I couldn't help but notice the lack of furniture and quiet atmosphere. The first voice I heard was a very harsh Japanese voice, "Take off shoes, please." It was Mr. Takenaka, the leader of the New Jersey MFT team, who was referred to as "commander."

I really didn't mind the military style leadership of MFT. I had grown up in a military family. In my home, in Pelham, we had a 30.06 military rifle mounted above Douglas MacArthur's speech "Duty, Honor, and Country." We would address our father as "sir" sometimes, though this tradition mercifully faded away over time.

When I was in grade school back in the 50's and 60's, before the age of digital programming, broadcast television would go off the air about 1 am. Every night's programming would end with music playing to a video of an F 104 while a poem entitled "High Flight" was read. It is a very moving poem written by a 19 year old World War II fighter pilot who was killed in battle three months after writing it. The original video still exists on YouTube. Many nights I would watch this video if I happened to still be awake, delaying going to bed until the last possible moment. There was no Facebook in those days. I thought of this poem and the idealism of this young airman as I joined MFT, not knowing what the future would bring.

> *"Oh, I have slipped the surly bonds of earth,*
> *And danced the skies on laughter-silvered wings;*
> *Sunward I've climbed and joined the tumbling mirth of sun-split*
> *clouds -*
> *and done a hundred things*
>
> *You have not dreamed of -*
> *and, while with silent, lifting mind I've trod*
> *the high untrespassed sanctity of space,*
> *put out my hand and touched the face of God."*

Anyone who tells you they like fundraising is a liar. It is the most difficult, unnatural thing to do. No one can do it for an extended period of time without tapping into a source greater than one's self. Call it God, Allah, the Force or call it whatever you like. In the Unification Church, MFT is called the front-line. It's about putting belief into practice, overcoming limitations and concepts about ourselves and how we relate to others. It's about extending the limit of physical and emotional tolerance to find where God really is existing in any situation. It's about uniting mind and body when the body is screaming, "No way, Jose." It's about overcoming physical desires for food, sleep and female companionship. It's about repairing the rift between God and Man by acting on our faith and finding where God is present, even in impossible or uncomfortable situations, inheriting his parental heart of love. It's about using the Divine Principle to solve problems both personal and public. It's about meeting people every day who may despise you, ridicule and mock you or worse, and not just once, but over and over again. It's about loving your enemy and bearing your cross, no matter what. Sometimes that meant putting yourself in situations where you may be vulnerable. You learn to forgive and to love.

> *"Let us go forth with the heart of the Father in the shoes of a servant, shedding sweat for earth, tears for mankind and blood for heaven."*
>
> Sun Myung Moon

Some people may think that, "Oh, the Unification Church is all about money" etc. Those people have no idea of the real motivation and experiences of most of those who fundraised on MFT. For me, it was never about the money. Yes, there were a few that practiced so called "heavenly deception." That is, they hid who they were raising funds for, presumably so they could make more money. I was not one of them. To be truthful, I was never asked to do it, nor would I if I had been. Those that did I view as fools or social climbers, maybe even criminals. They never understood the real value or purpose of MFT. The experiences I had, however, were invaluable. They showed me time and again the validity of the Divine Principle and the reality of God. God showed himself to me, not just on one occasion, but repeatedly.

I was not a good fundraiser. My personality is way too abrasive to be a good one. I have an Irish temper that can appear at any moment. I hate to see injustice being done. Sometimes, I would just have to calm down for a while if I or my church was ridiculed by some negative person. Usually, I would rather fight or argue than sell.

I did get better at it over time and learned to focus on reaching a goal. My goals were internal, spiritual goals. I would have an external goal too, but the internal goals like, "loving one's enemy", "perseverance", or "forgiveness" gave meaning and purpose to the day.

Numbers did have a lot to do with it though, and every day was an adventure to see how God was going to meet my goal, either internally or externally. One time I made $161 each day for six days consecutively. I can't think of any reason that this would happen and the odds of it are....

out there. It wasn't even my goal. All I know is that I counted what I made at the end of the day and that's what it was. Perhaps it was just God letting me know he is there and has everything under control. I have no other explanation. Sometimes he does that to me, it's almost like he has a sense of humor.

A few months ago, I was driving my limousine early in the morning, as usual. I was sent to 55 Hemenway St. in Shrewsbury, MA. Our area of business covers more than 50 towns in central Massachusetts. It's an area of perhaps 5 million people. Worcester, Massachusetts alone has more than 1000 streets. I set my GPS to 55 Hemenway and off I went. I arrived on the darkened street to where the GPS sent me and shined my flashlight on the house and it said 51. No biggie. I went back a few houses and pulled into the driveway of 55 Hemenway, not thinking anything of it. I picked up the customer and drove him to Logan airport. When I cleared with the dispatcher he told me to go to Terminal B and take a customer to Shrewsbury. Ok, back to Shrewsbury. That in itself was a little unusual but when the customer told me his address was 51 Hemenway I nearly fainted. I told him his grass needs to be cut and there are a few old newspapers in his driveway. I then told him I already had his address in my GPS as 55 Hemenway! I think he got a little scared at that point until I told him the whole story. He did not know his neighbor except in passing.

This is an unusual story too, but on MFT you came to expect the unexpected. Sometimes it just took a little courage or gall. One time, I was fundraising with candles and chocolates in an Hispanic area of Yonkers, NY in a manufacturing district. I have been in every kind of factory, machine shop, sweat shop imaginable from almost 2 years on MFT. This particular day I fundraised a sewing facility on the 3rd floor of a very large warehouse. There didn't seem to be anything going on in the 1st and 2nd floor but when I got to the third floor I saw perhaps 100 Hispanic women sewing curtains at sewing machines, a potential gold mine since this was payday. The women looked up when I came in the door, but I was immediately confronted by a very large, nasty foreman who proceeded to lay some NY swears on me at the top of his lungs, pushed me physically out the door and insulted me and the founder of our church with some spicy word enhancers. I dusted myself off and went back down to the first floor, thinking that there may be one or two people I could approach down there.

Unfortunately, there was no one on that level, but I saw an elevator and I went in it thinking that perhaps there was another area above. However, when the door opened I realized that I was now in the back of the same third floor area that I just got tossed out of. Several of the women saw me in the elevator and as they had just seen me get ruffed up, they were afraid for me, but they were laughing under their breath. The foreman was leaning on the first table with his arms crossed, looking out at the door in the opposite direction, perhaps waiting for me to try and sneak back in the front door. One of them motioned to me, so I scooted along the floor and hid under one of the curtains as she handed me 5 dollars. I hopped like this from sewing machine to sewing machine, quickly selling the contents of my box. They couldn't laugh out loud for fear of the foreman turning around and seeing me. I had one box of chocolates left and there was just one last sewing machine, the very one with the foreman leaning on it! I got low and dove under the curtain. She handed me the money. I had an empty box! I stood up and walked out the back and down the elevator. All those ladies blew me kisses or gave me a thumbs up. Some even clapped silently. I would have given anything to have seen that foreman's face when he turned around and saw every table with a candle or box of chocolates on it.

In another instance, I had a similar experience chasing a train as it was leaving the station. I threw boxes of chocolates up to the people as the train slowly accelerated. I finally caught up to the last person with outstretched arm and handed him the last box while he let the money fly out the window as the train disappeared.

On MFT we had a lot of time to study and read. I carried a copy of the six hour Divine Principle lecture, which I read over 100 times and committed to memory. I have read the full 536 page version 40 times over the years as well as scores of other books and materials. I have read the entire Bible twice, and have hundreds of verses committed to memory. I have also taken several courses in the Old and New Testament while at the Unification Theological Seminary. People who try to argue Bible verses with me are in for a rude awakening. Nevertheless, I have never found it helpful to quote Bible verses with Unification Church opponents. While on MFT I was constantly meeting people who would try to convert me with their Bible knowledge. Their arguments were always circuitous. Fundamentalists are not open to any interpretation of the Bible that conflicts with their doctrinal approach. Sometimes I just couldn't resist showing off a bit, but those kinds of discussions never left me with a good feeling.

Living in the New York area I got many chances to see and hear Rev. Moon speak as he spent a great deal of time there. He would speak every Sunday and at other occasions. The first time I got to meet him personally he bought me and several other members of my team new suits at Korvette's in New York. I remember the friendly and cordial way he helped each person find the right suit that fit just perfectly. I remember him straightening the shoulders out for me and I got a brisk slap on the back.

After a few months in Piscataway, our group transferred to the New Yorker Hotel, right in the center of Manhattan. Back then, the New Yorker was referred to as the World Mission Center. It was constantly full of people and was the center of what was happening in the Unification Movement worldwide. MFT occupied only one floor of the 40 story building. We would sometimes take a van to some area in Jersey or Westchester County in NY or at times we would just take the subway.

On my first day fundraising in NY I was dropped off at 166th Street and St. Nicholas Avenue and my area was the west side of St. Nicholas all the way down to 125th St. I had no idea where I was. I started going from shop to shop. The whole street was only black people, except for me of course. People were friendly but I occasionally got some strange looks from them. Finally, I came to this bar and was speaking to some of the patrons and the barkeeper came over to me and said, "Boy, don't you know where you is?" I said, "It's Manhattan," or some other dumb answer. He said, "No, boy, this here is Harlem. Now here's five dollars. I suggest you get your white ass out of here for your own safety." I left but kept on going shop to shop, grateful for the warning but undeterred. To me it didn't matter.

We fundraised in the worst areas of New York and New Jersey, sometimes until the wee hours of the morning. I encountered many situations where I could have been killed, but I can only say that God protected me on all those occasions. People would occasionally try to rob me. I found that most people, especially Hispanic or African American, have a deep religious sense buried inside them and I learned to appeal to that when I was cornered by gang members or thugs. I would tell them in a loud voice in English or Spanish that I was working for the church and that if he was going to take my stuff he was only taking from himself or from God. This tactic worked every time. Even the worst criminal types have a healthy fear of the Lord.

I saw so many heart wrenching and pitiful things in NY and Jersey. I witnessed a 9 year old who was a prostitute. After she approached me I saw her get picked up by a man passing in a car. I became sick to my stomach. There are so many people in our society that have serious mental health issues. Many of them are homeless and do not appear statistically in our society. When you walk the streets of NY like I did you see where they live and how they live. I also met many elderly people who were essentially abandoned by their relatives, living their last days alone. I sometimes talked to them as they often invited me into their apartments just to have someone to talk to for a while. I listened to their stories. Some of them had remarkable accomplishments. They gave me water or would sometimes feed me.

In January I received some new gloves for my birthday in the mail from my mother. I had some old gardening gloves but these were very nice and warm and fit perfectly. I was grateful to get them. The very day after I got them I went up to the Bronx to fundraise and was going shop to shop. One of the first places I visited was a pub that had maybe ten patrons at the bar and at tables eating breakfast. It was a bitterly cold morning. I was happy to have the gloves. I took them off when I went inside and put them in my pockets. Just at that moment a very old homeless woman came into the pub. She had obviously been sleeping on the street and begged the barkeeper to let her warm up in the bar for a few minutes. She was nearly frozen and covered with frost and ice. Not only did he tell her to leave but he and his patrons insulted, taunted and bullied this old woman to the point of tears. She said that her hands were frozen. I had never seen anything like this in my life. I gave her my brand new gloves and walked out.

You can tell from the lines on her face
You can see that she's been there
Probably been moved on from every place
'Cause she didn't fit in there

Oh, think twice, 'cause it's another day for you in me in paradise
Oh, think twice, it's just another day for you,
You and me in paradise, just think about it, think about it
　　　　　　　　　　　　Another Day in Paradise, Phil Collins

I fundraised the housing projects in the Bronx and in Brooklyn's Bedford/Stuyvesant, sometimes late into the night. There were endless rows of 20 story government owned apartment buildings, home to drug dealers, prostitutes, gang members, retirees, elderly, single mothers and simple working people. We would go in pairs. Usually, there were a few gang members hanging around the lobby. Many people were afraid to open their doors, but some did. There are amazing people wherever you go. We had a tactic to avoid the gang members. We would take the elevator to the top. Then we would run down the side stairs three or four floors and knock on doors on the 16th floor, then run down a few more flights to the 12th floor then take the elevator back up to the top. By then the gangs would give up looking for us. We could do about half the building that way and then we would run out the front door and onto the street and over to the next building.

Sometimes I was lucky enough to be paired up with Eldridge Wiltz, a former US Marine. A very friendly yet imposing figure, Eldridge looked like he could have been a defensive lineman on the New England Patriots. I was never afraid when around him. Just one icy stare and it was like the parting of the Red Sea.

We fundraised strip joints at night occasionally. I had never been in one of these places but if you stayed focused you could make a killing, especially from the dancers who liked flowers and candy and would give you tip money that was, well ...let's just say the bills were warm.

One of my favorite spots was the high rise apartments around Central Park, around where John Lennon lived. We would go by those spots late at night and just fundraise to the doormen and people on the street. It's a pleasant atmosphere over there in the summer and people are somewhat at ease.

I fundraised violin making factories, the Ford Plant in Mahwah, NJ., the Sikorsky Helicopter factory, Malls, shopping centers, and scores of traffic lights. I essentially hung out for three months at the traffic light across the street from Yankee Stadium. I once sold watermelon slices in Battery Park. I did the Staten Island Ferry, and every neighborhood in Long Island, Queens, Brooklyn, Yonkers, New Rochelle, Pelham and the towns along the Connecticut Border. I cannot think of a single town in New Jersey that I have not been in. In some small towns I did every house and building like Weehauken, Hoboken and West New York. I walked the entire 26 mile length of the Bergenline (not in one day) and did every single shop more than once. There are some places that are quite dangerous to walk through like Trenton, Camden and Newark. I did all that and came away basically unscathed, but with a few close calls.

In East Orange, NJ, a couple of guys from the Black Panther Party tried to kick me off a traffic light which they said was theirs. I had really no place else to go and since I got there first I refused to leave. They spit on me and pushed me around but I would not budge, but when they tried to push me in front of a moving tractor trailer truck I decided to take the rest of the day off.

I can't remember how many dogs I got bit by. It just went with the territory. Sometimes people would release their animals intentionally, other times they would sneak up on me and bite me from behind. Once I was chased by a German Shepard and escaped by jumping onto the back of a tractor trailer cab. It was covered with grease, of course, and I fell and cut myself on it quite badly. I got so I could tell which dogs were going to bite and which ones were just bluffing. If I did a house that was gated, I learned that you had better rattle the gate and call out for the dog first before going in. Waking him up while you are on the property was a sure way to get bit.

Some people have a gift for fundraising. They could easily make two or three times what I could do. Occasionally, I would be paired up with one of the best, Cathy Brown. Once we were given a 40 block strip of downtown businesses in New Jersey. She went down one side of the street and I went down the other side. When one of us got to the end he/she would cross the street and come back the other way. We would fundraise until we met up. Well I did my 40 blocks and came back the other side and met her finally after doing another 36 blocks. It took me all of 10 hours. It was a tough day. I had only made 40 dollars. I figured she must have taken the day off as she had only done 4 blocks in 10 hours, but she had made 400 dollars! It seemed impossible. We were saying the same thing to people, we had the same product, I was even wearing a tie! No matter. I felt like I had just wasted 76 blocks of area.

At night we would go bar to bar, sometimes until 2 am. At first I would just get kicked out of places. It was automatic. Usually I would go as a body guard for some of the better sister fundraisers, like Cathy. I would get kicked out of most spots in 2 seconds but she could stay for a half hour or even an hour in some of these places, making very large sums. Once I complained to her about it and she said, "Oh, Mark, I'm sure you'll do better in the next spot." Wouldn't you know it? The next spot I made over a hundred bucks! My good fortune ended, however, with one establishment. I just went back to being kicked out as usual. That's just the way it was.

Once I was inadvertently dropped off in a Jewish area on Yom Kippur of all days. My product, Christian jewelry pieces. I actually made 40 dollars that day, a miracle if you think about it. Some of the people would yell at me since on Yom Kippur Jews are not allowed to buy or sell. Others just gave me money because they admired my "chutzpah" which translated means "adventurous spirit."

Some of you may remember the blizzard of 78. The night before the storm hit I went to sleep as usual. We had no idea that there was the storm of the century about to hit the next day. I had a dream. In my dream I am walking along, and I hear horses' hoofs behind me. I turn around and there is Jesus on a white horse. I can hear the horse breathing and snorting as Jesus pulls the reigns on the horse, bringing it to a halt. Then Jesus removes a large silver sword from its scabbard and holds it high in the air in the light. The sword itself is giving off rays of light and energy. He then points the sword at me and I am enveloped in the energy of the sword. I then suddenly awaken, breathing quickly.

On MFT there were no snow days. We went out as usual, into the blizzard. I took the subway north all by myself as far as I could go and got off and went house to house. The snow was quickly becoming very deep, eventually two feet or more. Nothing was plowed and it was exhausting going house to house. I was constantly getting stuck and falling down. Finally, I came to a Lithuanian Orthodox Church. I wondered if it was open and perhaps I could take a break and sit down for a minute. The door was unlocked.

I went in and sat down in one of the pews for a few minutes to catch my breath. I had a feeling there was someone behind me. I turned around and there was a huge fresco on the back wall. It was a painted fresco of Jesus mounted on a white horse, looking straight at me with sword drawn, its rays of energy emanating outwards in every direction.

TROUBLE IN PARADISE

> *Hummingbird don't fly away, fly away.*
> *Hummingbird don't fly away, fly away.*
> *Haven't you noticed the days somehow keep getting longer?*
> *And the spirit voices whisper in us all.*
>
> *Haven't you noticed the rays? The spirit sun is stronger*
> *And a new day is dawning for us all.*
> *Hummingbird don't fly away, fly away.*
> *Hummingbird don't fly away, fly away.*
>
> Seals and Crofts, "Hummingbird"

By now I had been on MFT for several months. All this time I had written and called home a few times. I visited home on occasions like Thanksgiving and Easter. My parents were obviously upset with me for joining the church, but all I could do was try to be light and upbeat. I kept in touch with Jeanne by the occasional phone call. We saw each other sporadically. To be honest, I was really focused on what I viewed as a providential activity. My family, unfortunately, didn't see it that way.

Once I called the Boston Church and I was informed that Jeanne was struggling somewhat. I didn't know what it was about but she was not there at the time. I started to worry since the last time I saw her she seemed quite happy. Finally, we did talk on the phone and she said she wanted to visit with me. The last time we met was at the New Yorker Hotel. We spoke for quite a while and went out for dinner. As we talked I realized that we were going in different directions. I felt helpless to do anything about it. I knew in my heart that I would never see her again. After she left I cried for a couple of days. A few months later I received an annulment letter in the mail. I contemplated not signing it and contesting it in court, but I realized that this is what she wanted. With deep regret I signed the paper and sent it off in the mail.

This was such a shock to me. I never dreamed that I would be a divorced person. It's just something that never happened in our family. The pain of it was at times unbearable. Unless you have gone through it then you really have no idea. To be honest, I don't blame her as much as I do myself. I chose not to take time and communicate more often. People who know me know that I am Mr. Gung Ho at times. Now I really was a single member in the church, just like almost all the others, but I was feeling very much alone at times. This was not part of my original plan.

> *Suddenly I'm not half the man I used to be*
> *There's a shadow hanging over me*
> *Oh yesterday came suddenly*
>
> Lennon and McCartney

On the other hand, I was meeting all kinds of people, creating lifelong friendships. I was learning a lot about myself. I felt that I was doing things far beyond what I imagined could be done by anyone. I decided that the only way to overcome my doldrums was to invest myself even more in the activities that were inspiring to me. I continued on, knowing that God was present in the things that I was doing. I was in excellent physical condition and could run, climb stairs and carry heavy product boxes in 100 degree weather all day without difficulty. Also, since we were living in New York we often attended Sunday services and holidays, hearing Rev. Moon speak nearly every week. There was so much activity going on in the New Yorker, we were never bored. Occasionally, we went on trips to upstate New York to the towns surrounding Albany and Schenectady. These were welcome drives through some of the most beautiful country anywhere. We would stay in motels or sometimes in the Albany center.

By this time my circle of friends was becoming quite large. After 40 years as a church member I know thousands of members and when I meet them after having not seen each other in decades, these greetings are always full of tears, hugs, gratitude and great stories. The other day I met Mr. Takenaka and his wife Francoise. I had not seen him in over thirty years. I hugged him and kissed him on the forehead. The things we experienced on MFT were that profound.

Peter Perry, Mr. T and Mark at Belvedere
Celebration in 2016, MFTers from 1977

What I remember most about MFT life was the feeling of comradeship that was created through this common suffering activity. At the end of each day we shared our experiences with each other. I learned how to give a good back rub and got many as well, often from one of the Japanese brothers who knew shiatsu, a painful but relaxing stress relieving experience. We talked about our deepest struggles with each other and supported and encouraged each other through the good and bad days.

Altogether I was on the National MFT for one year and seven months. It was the most difficult thing I ever had to endure up to that point, but it was mere training for what was to come. Those who endured it for many years with a grateful heart and survived are saints. They are diamonds buffed to a perfect shape and gloss. Their faith and humility is beyond comprehension. They were living the Divine Principle to such a high degree that other members were jealous of them. If you walked through a group of Unificationists back in those days, you could pick out those who were on the MFT. They were tanned (if they were white), chiseled to be sure, but their faces had a gleaming bright spirit that was unmistakable. They were, in a sense, a living sacrifice. In the end, I was fortunate enough to marry one of the best and most faithful. My wife, Ursula, whom some of you may know, was on the MFT for 8 years. She received a service pin which very few accomplished. It's called the "white pin." It is considered one of the highest honors to have received one.

Leaving the MFT was something like getting off a roller coaster. Years later I taught in the public school in Pittsburg, NH. Those of you who are teachers know the feeling of the last day of school. Well, multiply that times 10, and that's pretty much how it felt.

My MFT life suddenly ended one day when a public memo was sent around that a new musical organization was forming called Sunburst II. The original Sunburst was on the west coast in California. This rock band was to perform mostly at the New Yorker in the Terrace Ballroom and at the Manhattan Center. The Manhattan Center was getting a makeover and the Terrace Ballroom, which was adjacent to the New Yorker, was being used several times a week for music performances to the public. I decided I would audition and the next day I found myself with several other musicians auditioning at the Belvedere Estate in the main living room. I hadn't played an instrument in almost two years and I was pretty rusty. Rev. Moon himself listened to our playing. There was one other guitar player, Joe Longo, auditioning in addition to myself. I was the superior player, but he was younger and a lot more energetic in his playing. I lost the audition. In retrospect, I often wondered what would have happened to me if I had won that audition. Sunburst II became the band of Hyo Jin Im, the eldest son of Rev. Moon. As Hyo Jin Im struggled with his demons later in life, I regret not having the chance to work with him. I'm not saying I could have done anything different to help him, but I would have liked the chance.

Instead, I got a consolation prize, which in retrospect, was a much greater blessing. It was the beginning of my life of travel. I was assigned to David Eaton and the Go World Brass Band, a church sponsored performing arts organization. They played jazz, pop, and marching stuff. They asked me if I knew how to play the bari sax. I had played a little alto sax in college in addition to clarinet.

My life on MFT officially came to an end. However, I didn't have to move anywhere since the band was stationed in the New Yorker. In the beginning of 1979, our basic witnessing outreach was called Home Church. Each of us had an assigned area in New York that we would visit and meet with people and teach them in their homes. My area was in Brooklyn off of Flatbush Ave. Most of the people were either Hispanic or Lebanese. We invited them to programs a couple of nights per week in the Terrace Ballroom at the New Yorker Hotel. It was fun playing on the same stage that Benny Goodman used to play on. There was one brother, Cesar Regalado, who was an excellent flute player. He and I learned a few Latin jazz pieces where I backed him up on the classical guitar. We played to many full houses. Sometimes Rev. and Mrs. Moon would come and sit in the audience. We played a few times at church holidays. I even played clarinet a few times with the New York City Symphony conducted by Kevin Pickard. These activities went on until the spring of 79.

CARP

> *Get your motor runnin'*
> *Head out on the highway*
> *Lookin' for adventure*
> *And whatever comes our way*
>
> Steppenwolf

The Collegiate Association for the Research of the Principle, or CARP is the collegiate outreach of the Unification Church. At the time of the writing of this book there is probably no college or university in the United States or the world for that matter that has not had a chapter on campus at one time or another. The spring and summer of 79 marked the beginning of a major outreach on college campuses. The members of the Go World Brass Band were assigned to CARP. We had several new vans for the band, so we loaded up our equipment and away we went. The campaign took us to Boston University, Harvard, City College of New York, Columbia and then down to the University of Florida, just as school let out. We marched, played in events, and witnessed. There were perhaps 500 members on this campaign on the East Coast and an equal number working on the West Coast. Our goal was to establish CARP on every campus in the US.

Part of the goal of Unificationism is to present a critique and counterproposal to Communism or Marxism-Leninism. It is a systematic and logical approach to the subject, not an emotional knee jerk reaction to it that others like the McCarthy era pogroms portrayed. As you can imagine, this idea became an anathema to organizations like the Students for a Democratic Society, the Black Panther Party and other similar groups. Wherever we went they would mobilize against us. They were determined to prevent us from establishing any foothold on campus. We were equally, if not more so, intent on doing just that. The confrontations we had with these people were intense and became physical quite often.

I got my first taste of one of these battles at Columbia University. We organized a rally and immediately a counter rally sponsored by several of the leftist factions on campus opposed us as we played music. When our speaker, Mike Smith, came to the microphone the opposition forces attempted to shout him down. Mike Smith, however, is one of the most powerful speakers and has a really big voice. At about 6'5" with a booming voice and sharp intellect, he is an intimidating figure to say the least. As the 100 or so leftists got closer to the microphone they attempted to take the microphone away by pushing past us onto the stage. We pushed back. One guy tried to take my bari sax so I cracked him in the side of the face with it. It quickly became a pushing and shoving match between two large groups.

At this point I have to tell you about Tiger Park, who was at that time the head of CARP. One of the earliest members to join in Korea, Chung Gu Park was short, but very powerfully built with a very tough looking weathered face. He also embodied the spirit of CARP. Having endured the Korean War and joined the church, he was one of Rev. Moon's most trusted followers. He, more than any other Korean that I have met other than Rev. Moon, showed me by example what it meant to be a Unificationist. The man was totally fearless, but a gentle man nonetheless. That being said, he was not someone that would compromise his ideals in the slightest, and had this fighting spirit that he always tried to instill in us. Unificationists are humble, religious people, but in this type of activity it was important to stand your ground and not be intimidated. We weren't.

As these two groups continued to push and shove each other, Tiger Park emerged out the group. It was like the parting of the Red Sea. Our opponents were clearly afraid of him. They didn't want to start anything with him especially. He was unafraid. He walked right into the middle of them and laid down. They were afraid to touch him. They thought he knew martial arts. Our opponents decided to call it a day. It was one of the bravest things I ever saw. The inherent danger of that moment is hard to convey. I was never so scared in my life, yet here is this guy with a big smile on his face defeating this huge group of bullies with just his presence and guts. I witnessed several incidents like this over the years.

A game of Yute with Tiger Park in Boulder, Colorado

Our band traveled across country from Florida to Colorado. Along the way we fundraised until we got to Boulder. We were to attend a CARP summer witnessing kick off campaign rally. I got my first look at the states of Alabama, Mississippi, Louisiana and Texas. I even got myself arrested in Garfield, Texas for fundraising without a permit. I spent a day in jail with some ruffians who had been arrested on various charges. They had been charged with stuff like possession of marijuana, indecent exposure and petty larceny. They asked me what I was in for. I replied, "selling candy for my church." One fellow's response was priceless. "Shit, you can't do nothin' no more." It was like a scene from "Alice's Restaurant." It wasn't a bad experience, though being led around in handcuffs is degrading and a bit frightening. It makes you feel very vulnerable. If you've ever been arrested you know what it feels like.

> *He was born in the summer of his 27th year*
> *Coming home to a place he'd never been before*
> *He left yesterday behind him, you might say he was born again*
> *You might say he found a key for every door*
>
> John Denver, "Rocky Mountain High"

500 or so of us stayed at a large facility at the University of Colorado. For a week we sang songs, played sports, climbed a 9,000 foot mountain in the Rockies, played Yute (a Korean game similar to Parchesi). We also planned a summer witnessing campaign in California.

That summer was jam packed with so many activities. First, we traveled the rest of the way by van to California, stopping in Salt Lake City to fundraise a bit, and then past the Great Salt Lake and through the moon like mountain deserts of northern Nevada, Reno, and finally arriving in Oakland, CA. We witnessed at Berkeley on Telegraph Ave. for a couple of days. I spent a day in San Francisco exploring. By then there were nearly 1000 members in Oakland. It was decided that we would split up into teams. Our team spent the remainder of the summer in Santa Cruz, a beautiful seaside resort town. It is one of the most picturesque, relaxing places in the world; the smell of eucalyptus trees, sandy beaches, 17 mile drive, Big Sur, pedestrian only downtown area with outdoor cafes playing live music almost 24 hours a day. Why would anyone want to go anywhere else?

Witnessing in that town, however, was really, really difficult. We got a lot of persecution from Fundamentalist Christian groups and leftist groups wherever we went. There were about 50 of us living in a very large house a few blocks from the beach. We tried to invite people for evening programs and workshops but with little or no result. After a few weeks Tiger Park came and lived with us to give us some inspiration, but the only people we got to respond were a few Hell's Angels. Back on MFT it was a lot easier to raise a few bucks than to witness to live people.

One sister from Wales, Liz Williams, suggested to Tiger Park that she would continue to witness day and night without sleep until she brought someone. She was not going to be allowed to go by herself as it was obviously too dangerous for one person alone. Tiger Park asked if some brother would volunteer to go witnessing together with her. I volunteered, not realizing what I was getting myself in for.

Liz and I witnessed one entire day talking to people without result. When the last van came in the evening to take everyone who was still out witnessing back to the center we just continued on. People were always out and about late at night in Santa Cruz and it wasn't difficult to find people to talk to until about 3 am. After three the streets were totally empty. The first night was the most difficult. We couldn't sit down because we would just fall asleep. We found a swing set at a park and the action of swinging on it was relaxing but would not allow you to doze off. Finally, day came and taking a shower and eating breakfast gave us new life. The second day seemed to go by much like the first. We didn't feel that tired but we still didn't get any result, meaning a guest to the center. So, another night went by much like the first. It's funny, but the second night didn't seem as difficult and we found a midnight café where we brought guests for coffee until the wee hours.

The third day went by. It was amazing to me that we didn't feel tired, but when you haven't slept for three nights you don't feel quite the same. It was very hard to pray as your mind would drift. Yet, both of us were determined to see it through. The fourth day I was beginning to waver a bit, but by this time not only Tiger Park, but True Father had heard of what we were doing and he ordered us to cease by the end of the fifth day, result or no. I can't remember a thing about the fourth night except that it was getting very difficult to focus.

> ***It ain't over till it's over.***
> Yogi Berra

Finally, the fifth day came. This was it. We had to bring someone today or else we would consider this condition a failure. We witnessed the whole day without success. With 10 minutes to go before the van came we got into a conversation with a Japanese tourist. He was very friendly and seemed somewhat interested to come over. Just at that moment a group of Fundamentalist Christians saw us and just pushed us aside to talk about their program and how we didn't believe in Jesus, etc. One big guy just elbowed me out of his way, pushing me aside and standing directly in front of me.

Usually we were nice to Christians and tried to talk to them and show them some respect and humility, but at this point there was no way I was going to let this big bully just push me out of there. I was tired and quite grumpy. I had had it. I picked this guy up by the shirt collar and pushed him into a wall. Right in his face I told him every nasty swear that I could think of and that if I ever saw him on the street again bad things would happen. The so called Christians ran away with me shouting spicy word enhancers. Then I composed myself and apologized to the Japanese tourist, who was totally in shock. We gave him a pamphlet and got on the van and went back to the center. That Japanese brother came over, went to the workshop and joined the church, really! Yogi Berra was right!

When I got back to the center there was a letter for me. It was from the Unification Theological Seminary. The letter said that I had been accepted as a student in the upcoming year's freshman class. Classes were to start in two days. My life was about to change.... again. But first I had to sleep.

SEMINARY LIFE

> *I got no deeds to do,*
> *no promises to keep.*
> *I'm dappled and drowsy and ready to sleep.*
> *Let the morning time drop all its petals on me.*
> *Life, I love you,*
> *All is groovy*
> "Fifty Ninth Street Bridge" by Paul Simon and Art Garfunkel

had forgotten I had filled out an application, but as I thought about it that morning I thought that maybe this would be interesting; Biblical Studies, advanced Divine Principle lecture training, a little slower pace for a change. It didn't take long to make up my mind. By that afternoon I was off to San Francisco Airport. I bought a ticket for New York at the ticket counter. I had not flown in a plane for many years and was looking forward to the flight. I was also still in witnessing mode. I looked at the people getting on the plane and thought about if I were to witness to someone who I would witness to. I got on the plane and sat next to the window and gazed out as the plane lifted off and San Francisco slowly slipped from view. I was sitting next to a young guy about my age who was very clean cut.

I thought I would just witness to this guy. I talked to him for a bit. He said he was going to study theology in upstate NY. Then I noticed he was reading a familiar looking book. What else, the Divine Principle! I punched him in the arm. His name was Rick Schwartz. He would become my roommate at the Unification Theological Seminary in Barrytown, NY.

To be honest, the Unification Theological Seminary was nothing like I expected it to be. It is a beautiful campus of hundreds of acres that sits right on the Hudson River. There were members from all parts of the world attending, some of whom had come off front line missions like myself and others who had various experience in church businesses or academic fields. Most of them were more academically inclined than I was. There were a few leadership type people there. That is, they had been in positions of leadership prior to coming to the seminary. I had never been in a leadership position in the church, but part of the training of the Unification Theological Seminary was to prepare future leaders in our young movement. I decided that I would do my best to study, a not so easy task as I found out.

The first thing you notice about the seminary is that it's quiet, extremely quiet, all the time. Even with 120 students there and faculty, the place is cavernous, yet interesting. The grounds are huge, with walking trails and open fields. You really have time to think, meditate and pray. Well, maybe kind of pray. To me it's easier to pray in an active, goal oriented activity than pondering points of theology. It was hard to adjust for a lot of us who had come off front line missions. Discussions became debates and debates produced tangent ideas that could go anywhere. Listening to professors, most of whom were not Unificationists, was very draining sometimes as their bad lifestyles and shallow world views made some of us very upset, including myself. At times I wondered why Rev. Moon had sent us here to learn from these people who obviously had almost no clue what we were about, much less the Divine Principle itself.

One of the professors I enjoyed though was Dr. Young Oon Kim, professor of Systematic Theology and Unification Theology. One of the original Unification Church members, she had been a professor of theology prior to joining the movement in the early 1950s. She was also one of the first three Unification Church missionaries that came to America in 1959. Her books are widely circulated and her classes were, well let's just say, she had a unique style. Very formal and extremely traditional, she came prepared with complete notes which she would read for 3 hours from behind the podium with white gloves in a soft, melodious, feminine voice that would send you off into outer space, especially at 8 o'clock in the morning. Staying awake in her classes was quite challenging. Everything was pretty much in her books anyways, but it wasn't her lectures that made the class.

You see, Dr. Kim was a sucker for a good piece of cheesecake, and a few of us would take her out on Thursday nights nearly every week to the Culinary Institute of America in Hyde Park where the student chefs would create pastry delights for three bucks. There, she told us stories of how she wrote her books, early days in the church, theological stuff, and of course her understanding of the spiritual world. This woman was amazing. Like many Koreans of her era, she had many spiritual experiences, some of which she conveyed to us. Her books really are special. According to her, the people that she wrote about, whether Emil Brunner, Paul Tillich, or Augustine, each came to her to insist they include such and such an item or discuss their theories. Yet, her unique understanding made her interpretations of their works and theories palatable and meaningful. Studying theology is like walking through mud, but her books are so clear and insightful.

We studied the Old Testament with a Jewish Rabbi, the New Testament from a Protestant Pastor, and Church History from a Greek Orthodox church historian. The staff was very diverse and featured a Harvard Divinity School professor, a Chinese professor of Oriental Philosophy, a Catholic Priest who taught psychology and other professors from various denominations, in addition to Unificationist professors. Some of the courses were quite difficult. Also, a lot of theology is incomplete and full of dead ends. The things that became doctrine throughout history were based on false assumptions and antiquated thinking. Listening to this stuff day after day can bring you down since none of the ideas of Plato, Aquinas and Ockham are in themselves complete. The same thing holds true for Freud, Maslow and Jung or any of the other theories of psychology. Studying these guys is like doing mental gymnastics. It can also make you into an atheist if you're not careful. We had quite a few heated discussions with our professors over these theories. Sometimes I asked God why he had sent me to this cerebral place.

When I first joined the church I had a dream that stuck with me. Most of the dreams I have I forget as soon as I wake up, but this one made an impression on me. In my dream I was walking down a hallway when suddenly someone said to me, "Come on, let's go, Father is here." I followed a few people down this hallway until we came to a door guarded by a Korean man. He let a few people into the brightly lit room. When I got to the door he grabbed my shirt sleeve for a second, looked into the room and said, "Ok, go!" I went into the room. The sunlight came through tall windows illuminating the room in warm rays of light. There was brown wooden paneling and a long formal style dining table with high backed chairs. Rev. Moon sat at the head of the table and almost everyone else sat on the floor. Rev. Moon then spoke about the end of Communism.

By the time I had been in the seminary for three months I had been in every single room on campus. Every room, that is, except one. It was an unmarked room near the laundry room on the first floor facing the Messina house. No reason to go in there, I just never noticed the door until one day I was walking down that hallway on the first floor, when a few of the brothers passed me and said, "Come on, let's go, Father is here." I followed the others down the dark hallway until we got to the door. When I saw Rev. David Kim, the president of UTS, standing in front of the door, I thought to myself, "No way, this can't be." Rev. Kim let the others go in front of me, then grabbed me by the shirt sleeve, looked into the room and said, "Ok, go." By now you can fill in the rest. I do not know how this could have happened. All I know is that it did. I can tell you I had never been in this room before. Since then, every time I go to Barrytown I visit that room and remember that incident from way back in 1979. A few months ago, someone posted a photo of this very same meeting on Facebook. It's also interesting to note that Rev. Moon spoke of the end of communism. I was to witness the end of communism first hand in the Soviet Union many years later.

Lesa Ellanson, pictured prominently in the photo was in charge of horseback riding instruction for Rev. Moon's children. He wanted to know about her health situation, something he was frequently concerned about. This photo is reprinted with her permission

Rev. Moon came to the seminary 17 times while I was there. Most of the time he took us fishing in the lagoon. Fishing at the Seminary with Rev. Moon was not what you might imagine. A few years before I went to UTS Rev. Moon came to initiate a training program by teaching students how to fish the" Korean" way. Barrytown, NY is on the Hudson River. Just north of the school is a large lagoon whose only inlet is under a rail bridge perhaps fifty feet long. The Hudson River at Barrytown is affected by tides. At high tide the lagoon is several feet deep but at low tide it is knee deep at most, at which time 90 percent of it is just mud. The idea was to place a net perhaps 200 feet long blocking the entrance at high tide, leaving the fish stranded in low water and mud during low tide. These fish we would gather by hand with nothing more than our bare hands. Almost all the fish were river carp, a prized fish in Asia, but a nuisance fish in America. They are beautiful, huge goldfish, multicolored and very powerful. The fish that we caught we transferred to a holding tank and placed in the large pond at the seminary near the athletic field. Just as in the time of Jesus, this fishing was training to make us fishers of men.

Rev. Moon himself had made the net by hand, which he did over many days. The first time we did this activity he spent several hours repairing the holes in the nets made from the previous year. Catching these fish was no easy task. Old clothes that covered the entire body and some old sneakers were a necessity. The idea was to herd the fish into the low water until they got into the mud. To catch them there was a trick. If you put a thumb or finger into its mouth it would proceed to suck on your thumb and go into a trance, at which time you could reach under it and pick up the 10 pound fish, all the time keeping it sedated by leaving your finger in its mouth. The instant you removed the finger, the fish would wake up and wiggle out of your grip. As you can imagine, while doing this you are going to get wet and covered with mud from head to toe. You were going to fall or lose a shoe just like the principal in "Ferris Bueller's Day Off." Not only that but there were these tiny water thistles called "devil's heads" that would constantly stab you and get into your shirts or shoes. They had very sharp spikes and were everywhere. Also, who knows what else was in that water?

I had fished quite a lot as a child, so I didn't mind picking up slimy fish. I actually caught the first one that day. Holding a huge sleeping fish, it felt like a baby with a baby bottle. It was a fun activity once you got into it. The hardest part of it was setting the net poles. Sometimes we had to do this at night, not an easy task when the temperature was 35 or 40 degrees and the water just a bit higher than the 10 foot poles. That meant you had to dive down a few feet and set the poles into the ground while under the water. I'll admit after doing that a couple of times I found ways to avoid that task.

THE MATCHING

> *At three, I started Hebrew school. At ten, I learned a trade.*
> *I hear they've picked a bride for me. I hope she's pretty.*
> *The Papa, the Papa! Tradition!*
> *The Mama, the Mama! Tradition!*
>
> "Tradition", from Fiddler on the Roof

Driving a limousine in Massachusetts, a large portion of people that I pick up are immigrants from India. They are everywhere in this high tech rich area. They are doctors, computer techs, engineers and business entrepreneurs. When I speak with them I inevitably find out that the majority of them who are married met their spouses via matchmaker. They are successful, loving parents who create excellent families and are a boon to the communities in which they live. Their children are smart, hardworking and focused. This tradition is a part of many cultures throughout the world. In America, parents largely have a laissez faire attitude about their children's love lives. Sometimes these marriages are successful. Nowadays, most of the time they are not.

Unificationists don't date. I never dated since joining the church. I learned to see all women as my sisters. Could I date my sister? This is the amazing sense of freedom that young Unificationists feel. I was never in competition with anyone to win the affections of some girl. I am free. I learned to trust God in this matter. It took a while but he did come through for me. I got the right one.

The Unification Church is one big giant rumor mill. People constantly talk about stuff. What Father Moon is doing, what's the latest project, so and so has this problem or that problem. It's endless. Back in the 70's the most prevalent rumor was about the matching. When is it coming, where and how is it to take place, and so forth. In reality no one knew, so it was better to not think about it and just focus on whatever your job was. We knew, however, that the day would eventually come. Finally, the day did come, like a thief in the night. We got only two days' notice. There were 2000 qualified applicants. The date was December 30th, 1980.

Imagine the Grand Ballroom of the New Yorker Hotel, New York City; beautiful, amazingly well lit by crystal chandeliers, carpeted, and fantastically ornamented. It was the scene of many of Rev. Moon's speeches. I had been in the room countless times. We sat on the floor as usual, men on the right, women on the left. The room became very full and I mean full.

This matching ceremony obviously was going to take many hours, but, actually, I was there only ten minutes, an amazing fact considering I had a three-hundred-pound guy sitting in my lap and squashed in on all sides. I wondered if God could even see me. The first thing that Father Moon did was stand up all the men from the seminary in a line. The next thing I knew I was being pulled by the suit collar and this beautiful young blond from Germany and I were sitting at a table introducing ourselves and talking to each other for the first time. "Allo, I'm Ursula." That's how it was, really! That day Rev. Moon matched 843 couples. Ursula and I were number 34.

Ursula and Mark, December 30th, 1980, Day 1

We talked it over for maybe five minutes. That's it. Here I am, thirty-seven years later, telling you this story. Did it work for everybody, no. Did it work for me and most of the others that went on to get married later? Yes. I think the main reason it worked for me is that Ursula and I knew from the very beginning that we shared essentially the same spiritual values that are inherent in successful families. That was evident to both of us. It had almost nothing to do with what our personal preferences were in regard to this or that hobby or social preferences. We knew that those things would be worked out later. That night I sat for hour after hour looking at the picture that she gave to me of herself.

> *I never knew love before, then came you, then came you*
> Dionne Warwick and the Spinners

Seminary life after the matching was becoming quite difficult. I just wanted to get back out into the field and do something. On top of that I would daydream about my new sweetheart. Ursula was sent to MFT and we wrote and called each other occasionally. Sometimes she came up to UTS to visit. Studies were somehow taking a back seat. My mind was not easily focused at that point. I felt that I was vegetating and easily distracted.

Towards the end of my second year I really felt I had been there too long. Studying became an almost impossible chore. One of the things we did to pass the time was to play some basketball. Every evening we would play for an hour or so. Someone got the bright idea to join the local men's basketball league in Kingston. We formed our own team and performed adequately, much to the surprise of the locals. It was fun and we did win a few games against some pretty good competition. UTS had some pretty incredible athletes in 1980. We had quite a few guys who were from Europe and South America who could really play soccer. Soccer was not my thing. They challenged West Point to a soccer duel and beat them!

My favorite diversion was the pool table in the recreation room. There was an excellent pool table there and we had nightly matches. I had played quite a bit before the church. My own father was a pool hustler and he often paid for Christmas gifts with money that he would win in pool halls. At the seminary there was always a few guys playing and every night we went there when our studies were finished. I honed my skills and could beat anyone most nights. I once went to a pool hall with my dad many years later and beat him soundly, much to his chagrin. There was one person, however that no one could beat. His name was Sun Myung Moon. Once he came to the seminary and we organized a pool match. It's not that he had this great technique or anything. It's just that he got every break and advantage that came his way. I should have beaten all of them easily, but somehow the balls just would not go in! I couldn't hit the broad side of a barn. I lost in that tournament quite badly. It was fun, though, despite my bruised ego.

Pool Tournament at the Seminary

Nevertheless, I was really looking forward to graduation. It couldn't come soon enough as far as I was concerned. I felt that God's providence was somehow passing me by as I languished at school. One lazy warm spring day I was taking an afternoon nap, something that I would do after a long day of classes. Some brother came barging into my room and shouted, "Father is here, wake up let's go down to the pond!" I laid there with my eyes open for a couple of minutes and slowly walked over to the sink and splashed some water on my face. Looking in the mirror, I noticed how tired looking I had become the last few months. I slowly walked out of the building and meandered down the path thinking how much I didn't want Father to see me looking so tired and worn out. I walked slowly on with the thought that everyone else is probably already down there. I'll just sneak in the back unnoticed and keep my head down. I did have my head down as I walked down the bank towards the pond when, to my surprise, I saw True Father there at the pond all by himself! I was the first one there!

Too late now to go back, I felt totally ashamed being the only one. I felt like I was naked. All I could do was sit down in the grass next to Father with my head down. Father took one look at me, paused, and said, "Studying is like torture." I shook my head and thought, "Now here is someone who really understands me." I mumbled, "Yes sir Father, you got that right." Later, when I reflected on it I thought of how incredible it was that Father is someone who really understands what torture is, having experienced the worst kind of torture many times by the Japanese and North Koreans, comparing my situation to torture. He was actually comforting me in this pampered, Ivy league style of existence. I redetermined that I would finish out the last few months at UTS with a good heart.

Unification Theological Seminary, Class of 82

120 DAYS

> *It's a long road to freedom*
> *A winding steep and high*
> *But when you walk in love with the wind on your wings*
> *And cover the earth with the songs you sing,*
> *The miles fly by*
>
> "Long Road to Freedom"

ell, graduation wasn't what we expected. What we were expecting was to be sent off to some far corner of the world and work in some mission related field. What we got was another four months of school. Not just any school, but 120 days workshop taught by the Church's oldest and trusted disciples at the New Yorker Hotel. Great under normal circumstances, but just having been dragged through 2 years of seminary, sitting in classes all day for a third of a year was not what I had planned on. I'm sorry to say that my attitude during those four months was not exemplary, but it was good to hear the testimonies and the Principle as it was taught by the early followers, Ken Sudo, Won Pil Kim (first disciple of Rev. Moon), Rev. Chung

Hwan Kwak and several others. Getting to talk to them made us feel that we were part of the inner circle, well, almost.

Most of us, especially the seminarians were biting at the bit at that point. We played basketball in the afternoons as a diversion. One of the brothers had acquired a TV, and in the evenings, we hung out on the 31st floor, trying in vain to get some good reception. One evening that same brother, Terry Blount, noticed that on the floor below us was Father's apartment where there was a balcony with a small terrace overlooking the city. We also noticed that there was a cable running up the side of the building and into a window in the apartment, obviously a television cable. We needed some cable to get some good reception. One of our theological precepts was engrafting to the messiah, a very important part of the salvation process as some of you well know. Well, what better way to engraft than to connect to the cable of the man himself. We tied several bed sheets together and lowered Terry over the side of the 31st floor window so he could rappel down the 15 feet or so to the terrace. Our plan worked perfectly except that Rev. Moon's housekeeper saw Terry and assumed he was a terrorist/assassin, something that Rev. Moon's security people had already dealt with several times in the past. In about a minute they were pounding on our door, none too happy. We had to explain the whole thing to Mr. Sudo, but I think after that at least he understood where the seminarians were coming from and how we viewed this whole 120 day thing.

10 DOLLARS AND A BUS TICKET

If you should hear a song
Out in the meadow loud and clear
Have no fear he is there
Calling his children near

As time is the sunshine, wisdom is the key
His children are growing to be free
And in that land where He was King
He now a Bridegroom shall be.

"If You Should Hear a Song" by Sara Towe

After the 120 days workshop we were sent out to campuses throughout the United States. I worked for three months as director of CARP at Boston University where we witnessed and tried to build up the center in Allston. Then my mission suddenly changed and I was to be the state director of the Unification Church in Indianapolis, Indiana. After meeting with the members in Chicago and staying there for a week I got on a bus and away I went to Indianapolis. All I had was 10 dollars in my pocket. There had been a center in Indianapolis, but the few members who were there had been sent out either to CARP, or as overseas missionaries. I was in the city, totally alone in the dead of winter with no money. The first night I slept in the bus station. In the morning I bought myself breakfast at MacDonald's and stashed my stuff in a storage locker. I walked around the city for about an hour or so.

Indianapolis in 1982 was not the friendliest of cities. Like most Midwest cities it was not pedestrian friendly. People went everywhere by car. It was hard to meet people on the street. The ones that would talk to me were either homeless or drunks. Nevertheless, I had this feeling of ownership of the place and I was determined to make the most of it. This was my town.

In order to survive, much less witness, I needed to make some money. By now I was down to 7 dollars. I found a wholesale candy dealer and spent my last 7 dollars on a small case of chocolate bars. It took me about four hours to sell them. I now had 28 dollars. I bought myself a late lunch and went back to the candy wholesaler and bought another two boxes for 14 dollars. By eight pm. I had about 60 dollars. That was enough for one day so I went back to the bus station to sleep. Fortunately, I found someone who was leaving town that evening who had a key to a hotel room that he didn't need so I got a place to sleep for the night and I didn't have to spend any of my 60 bucks. I woke up in the morning refreshed and showered.

I needed a more permanent place to sleep at night until I could raise enough money to rent a room. I went to the Salvation Army and checked myself in with all the rest of the men who stayed there. Most of them were homeless drunks, former criminals and people who had just given up on life for various reasons. Like the others I was allowed to stay for three nights and then I needed to move on. After checking in I fundraised for the day. I did pretty well and by now had nearly 200 dollars. The weather was at times very nasty and I decided for the next few days to go to some of the places in town like libraries, museums, universities and learn the local bus system and what the neighborhoods were like. I fundraised a little each day and was saving more and more. Finally, I got booted out of the Salvation Army. I felt so sorry for the men who have to stay in those places with no hope in their hearts for something better. I couldn't really witness to them.

Some days I walked to a park on the south side of Indianapolis. Every state in the United States has a park that was visited in 1965 by Rev. Moon when he first came to America. Each of these parks is designated as a "Holy Ground". There is an unmarked tree (some of the trees are no longer living) and a spot where Rev. Moon prayed for that state. There is also a small piece of earth taken from the original holy ground in Korea buried there. It was a good place to pray and meditate or read.

I needed a better place to stay. I responded to an ad in the newspaper for a room in a house. The woman was very nice and agreed to let me live there, but it was too far from downtown and a little too restrictive. I eventually got a room at a boarding house about 15 blocks from downtown. I stayed there for about a month or so. It was cheap, convenient and clean. I did, however, witness a few tragedies there. My neighbor, who was quite elderly, died of a heart attack one evening. A few weeks later I saw another young man who lived there get struck by a car and killed.

Our church did own a building in Indianapolis. It had been the state center but then MFT took control of the house at 404 East 38th St. By 1982 MFT had no more need for the house and I inherited it after having been pioneering in Indianapolis for 40 days.

The house is quite large. Way too big for one person, but it was a lot better than living in the flophouse, so I took on this restorational challenge. The house had been abandoned for almost a year before I got there. There were mice everywhere and it was very dirty, and had almost no furniture. The house was supposed to be heated by oil but I couldn't afford to fill up the huge oil tank. I did notice that this old home had a coal room that was still 3/4 full of coal that had been sitting there perhaps 50 years. I started a wood fire in the chamber and threw in a shovel full of coal. Voila, heat. I don't think the neighbors appreciated the coal smoke, but I was able to heat the house for the entire winter and had enough for half the next winter.

There was an abandoned yellow 1975 Mustang sitting in the yard that needed some work. I claimed the car and started working to restore it. After about a week I got it running. It took another week to get a plate and title and insurance, but it was a good set of wheels. Now I could do some serious fundraising and witnessing.

The weather was improving and I would go downtown and street lecture to passersby with a small portable chalkboard. I made up a flyer and had business cards made up. I didn't get many guests this way, but it felt good to be teaching the Principle to people, if only in small sound bites.

People would occasionally stop and listen. It was good practice even if there weren't many to talk to.

I would go to Butler University and run a mile or two around the track every morning in the spring to stay in shape. I learned to cook a few dishes, mostly stir-fried vegetables and soups with rice. I did find three new center members eventually and reconnected three members who were living at home. It was good to have at least a small group to support the center and do activities. We visited other churches as well as universities and eventually went around the entire state, sometimes fundraising, sometimes witnessing. Once we went to 10 cities in one day to pray and establish holy grounds. Our day trip took us to Marion, Fort Wayne, Lafayette, Gary, Terra Haute, Evanston, New Albany, Columbus and Bloomington and a couple of others I can't remember.

I found the people of Indiana to be kind, decent and hardworking. Many where quite religious, though they tended to be on the fundamentalist Christian side. It was quite difficult, even for me, to talk to them in a coherent way. I became somewhat familiar with the breadbasket of the U.S.

During this time I had only a few conversations with Ursula and only the occasional letter. I knew that she was busy. I already knew what MFT was like. By now it was early 1982. The Blessing was being planned. It was to be on July 1st, 1982 at Madison Square Garden in New York, which was only a few months away. It would be the largest wedding in human history.

THE BLESSING

> *Yeah, yeah, yeah, hey, hey, hey. What about love?*
> *I've got a yearning in my heart, too,*
> *Yeah, yeah, yeah, hey, hey, hey. Here is my love;*
> *I'd like to give this song of love to you.*
>
> *Please let me in, when you're singing your song.*
> *I can't sit quiet; I just have to sing along.*
> *So, if you give one of yours, I will make it my own;*
> *It will be the sweetest song you've ever known.*
>
> "What About Love" by Kristina Seher

It was the wildest, happiest, craziest day of my life. There were 2075 couples, many of whom I knew, all married at the same time in the same ceremony. These were all my best friends, people I had worked and suffered with. At the time it was a world record and was recorded as such in Guinness's Book of World Records. Madison Garden was filled to capacity. The news coverage of it was broadcast worldwide. The other day I visited MSG to attend and sing in a 2000 voice choir at an event entitled "Peace Starts With

Me." Right at the front door there is a marble column commemorating the event back in 1982.

1982 Holy Blessing Ceremony, permanently engraved
in this pillar in Madison Square Garden

The rehearsal for the event the day before took nearly the entire day. The spirit and expectation were so high that no one could sleep the night before. Who can forget Dan Fefferman's version of "What About Love" that we all sang together that afternoon? I had purchased a very high quality suit. Putting it on that bright morning was the proudest day of my life up until that point.

Every room in the New Yorker Hotel the night before was booked. The place was absolutely crazy. I told Ursula I would meet her in the lobby at the designated time, but when the elevator doors opened all I could see was a sea of white wedding dresses and veils with a lot of bewildered looking guys trying to find their brides. It was so loud in there. I thought to myself, "Oh well, here goes," and started lifting veils and shouting out my wife's name. After about ten minutes I found her.

Mark and Ursula Hanlon marriage blessing photo, July 1st, 1982

As the 2075 couples walked across 8th Ave. over to Madison Square Garden, traffic came to a complete stop. Everyone wished us well and congratulations. The wedding itself was presided over by Rev. and Mrs. Sun Myung Moon. For those of us who participated it was a dramatic and life changing experience, unique to be sure, but to be honest it took me a while even after the ceremony to realize its huge value. To Unificationists, the wedding is more than just two people getting married, but is a milestone of spiritual significance. Some of us had already reached that milestone. For myself, it was several years later that I came to realize what that was and how valuable the Blessing really is. I'm not saying that I became worthy, but

I felt the value and the presence of God in the Blessing in a way that was very special. I felt at on the one hand how precious a gift it is, but at the same time, how vulnerable, hurt and in a way, powerless God was because of the Fall. The blessing is a kind of vindication for God, who has been trying to find his lost children for thousands of years, so that he could bestow his greatest gift upon them.

I have to say that, truthfully, I am a stubborn, arrogant at times and insensitive spouse. I also expected the church to do everything for me. I was wrong, and just continued in my mission, thinking that Ursula and I would just get together by some official decree. That day never arrived. I think that a lot of the couples that broke up after the Blessing was for that very reason. I didn't realize the authority that the Blessing itself has until years later.

I still had hope that someday this situation would resolve itself. It was very hard to continue day after day, but all I could do was discipline myself and keep as strict a schedule as I could and just practice living for the sake of others, simple Divine Principle. One of the things I did was visit television and radio stations. Our church had received so much media because of the Blessing event that local media people were eager to have me on for interviews. I did several of them. We also got some attention from churches that wanted to interview me and universities that had courses in modern religious movements. Even though we didn't get any direct result from this activity I felt it was worth the effort and we got a few allies in the religious, academic and media world. I also contacted the new CARP center at the University of Indiana in Bloomington and we did some joint projects. The Indianapolis center was becoming quite active. I was happy in the activities that we were doing.

I also got to fly to NY to go to Belvedere or East Garden (Rev. Moon's home in NY) every month for a few days with the other state directors. It was good to meet my coworkers and share ideas and hear reports from the field, as well as interact with Father Moon on a monthly basis. I looked forward to those meetings and I felt that though it was a suffering course that we were progressing in a way, getting a few new members and reaching out to the community in a variety of ways. I made friends with a few ministers from other faiths. Sometimes, I would invite them out for a Korean dinner.

Inspiration can come from the most unlikely of places. I found that sometimes you just have to stretch your imagination and not be afraid to experience new things. The center at East 38ᵗʰ St. is right on the borderline between the predominantly black area to the south and the wealthy white area to the north. Most of our contacts came from the south of East 38ᵗʰ St. but the closer you got to downtown the area became very seedy and somewhat dangerous, at night especially. About half way to downtown there was a restaurant called Big Mama's House of Soul Food. When you went by you could smell the most incredible barbeque smell. I wanted to go in there to eat, but it was always surrounded by hoodlums and seemed more like an ideal place to get mugged. One brother kept taunting me to go in there because I would always comment on how good that food smelled. One day he and I went in for a late lunch.

We were the only ones in the restaurant. We were greeted by this absolutely huge woman with an equally large smile. She put us at ease right away and helped us with our order as I had never had soul food before. We had barbeque with collard greens, black eyed peas, okra and a few other vegetable sides that I did not know what they were. The food was delicious, even if it was high calorie. At the end of the meal I asked her if she was the owner of the restaurant. She replied, "Do you mean, am I Big Mama?" I said shyly "Well ah, yes, uh, are you Big Mama?" She pointed to the kitchen and said, "No, that's my Mama." I didn't notice her at first, but you know how restaurants have this narrow slit maybe 5 feet wide where the cooks push the food through to the dining room. Well, this woman took up the whole 5 ft. wide slit. She had to have been at least 500lbs. She couldn't possibly be alive today. We went back there quite a few times. It was a friendly place to eat and hang out, despite the neighborhood. I looked it up on the internet the other day. It's still there.

There were two brothers from CARP that I became friends with and I went over there occasionally to help them with programs. They also came to Indianapolis, sometimes just to hang out and play ping pong. The Indiana center was becoming quite active and we always had something going on. We fixed up the center some, painted, and bought some new furniture. It started to look and feel more like a home. My doldrums seemed to fade away a bit. Occasionally, I went down to Kentucky to visit with my old seminary friend, Terry Blount, who was the state leader down there.

In the Unification Church nothing stays the same for very long. On January 1ˢᵗ, 1983, there was a state directors meeting at Belvedere as usual.

The meeting was essentially over when True Father put 50 numbers into a hat and numbered the states one through fifty. Each state leader was given a number. I got number 6. Number 6 was Montana. He told us to go directly to our new state and not go home. There were a few who did go to their new state directly, but all I had was 20 bucks and a return ticket to Indianapolis.

There was one brother who wanted to come to Montana with me but in the end he decided to stay in Indianapolis. The new state leader of Indianapolis came by his own car, so I prepared to leave for the Missoula, Montana center, where there were no members at all. I was a pioneer, again.

BIG SKY

> *Oh Montana, give this child a home*
> *Give him the love of a good family and a woman of his own*
> *Give him a fire in his heart, give him a light in his eyes*
> *Give him the wild wind for a brother and the wild Montana skies*
> "Wild Montana Skies" by John Denver

The next day I loaded up the 75 Mustang and went off to Montana, the Big Sky State. I had never been in the Pacific Northwest and I was excited about the opportunity to see a buffalo or antelope. It was however the dead of winter. It is an exhilarating drive from Denver to Missoula, going along the Rocky Mountains, past the Grand Tetons and Yellowstone, winding along the mountain river route on US 90 until you get to Missoula. Fortunately, there was no bad weather, and I checked into the center after a day and a half drive. The first thing you notice about Missoula is the smell of woodstoves. The center itself had no heat except for the woodstove in the center of the apartment. I lit it up and went to sleep.

People in Montana are quite different from those in the Midwest and South. In Indiana, Kentucky and Texas people tend to see everything as a social event. Definitely churchy, Midwesterners are very outwardly friendly and kind. Texans will generally socialize with you until you can't take it anymore. Not so in Montana. Montanans are generally reserved, quiet and meditative. It's easy to understand why. In Montana there are an average of 2 people per square mile. There are vast open spaces of big sky, and mountains as far as the eye can see in any direction. In some parts of Montana, you can drive for more than an hour and not see a single house, telephone pole or manmade structure, not to mention another car coming in the other direction.

In this kind of place, people tend to find inspiration in nature more than in the Bible. They have a kind of natural theology. Many of them are rough, hardworking, and have a sense of self-reliance and confidence in themselves. To them, they are living in heaven. They don't have a lot of questions about life. There is a large percentage of American Indians there, and native American religion plays a big role in the way people think and act. There are churches in Montana, but it didn't seem to me that the church played as much a part of their lives. They were kind of like people in New Hampshire, but more spiritual. They seemed more interested in you the person than what you represented. I found them very sincere and thoughtful, but they would prefer not to talk about religion.

On the other hand, Montana was a great place to fundraise. I could easily make 400 to 500 dollars a day selling just about anything. They didn't care what you were selling. They were just happy to see someone come to their corner of the world and would buy anything you had. I would drive for two or three hours to one town of say a thousand people and sell a picture and in about ten minutes half the town would come over to wherever I happened to be, or they might phone someone and send me down the road. The product would just sell itself. I would chat for a few minutes, check out the interesting spots in the town and drive home. I was making 1500/ week easily, fundraising 3 or 4 days per week.

After I had been in Montana for about a month or so the United States church got a lot of new volunteers who came from overseas to help in our witnessing effort. The first ones who came were from Japan. The five sisters who were initially assigned to Montana came to the regional headquarters in Seattle. I had never been to Seattle before and went there to greet them. Missoula to Seattle is one of the most spectacular rides you can imagine. The topography of Idaho and eastern Washington is very special and unique. The views and mountain terrain are stunning. Coming into Seattle through the mountain passes of the Cascade mountains and Mount Ranier was exhilarating.

When I met the new Montana members I quickly realized that not one of them could speak English, at all! I took a few of them in the Mustang and the others came a few days later by bus. Our center now had myself and 5 Japanese women, none of whom I could communicate with. I had a lot of money by this time in the church account so we were alright there for a while, but what was I supposed to do? I learned that the great trait of the Japanese is to be able to adapt and thrive in any situation. They worked together so well and quickly made themselves known throughout the community. We started to have many guests, especially from the University of Montana. They just invited people to the center for a Japanese dinner and we would give them a lecture. It worked quite well and we got some guests for advanced study in Seattle.

I got recruited to be the 7 days workshop lecturer in Seattle. I have to say that of all the workshop places that I went to, the Seattle lakeside house called Windemere is the most beautiful. Sitting on several acres of land on Lake Washington's western shore, from the front balcony you can see magnificent Mount Ranier rising in the distance on the opposite shore. This spectacular workshop retreat would inspire anyone just by the environment. It was very relaxing for me to teach there for a couple of months. We taught several people who joined and it rejuvenated me as well. I did have to go back and forth to Missoula quite often to take care of matters there and to cart members around. I must have made that 9 hour trip ten times in all. Sometimes I did fundraising as well.

There is incredible nature in Montana. It really is God's country. Sometimes, though, he must feel he needs to use it to teach us to be humble. The weather there is unique as I found out on May 10th, 1983. It was a spectacular day. 70 degrees, blue sky. I took my Mustang out to do a quick fundraising trip to Havre, a small town on the Canadian border. I left in the morning to drive the 2 and a half hours. I passed many antelope, cattle and prairie dogs. There were huge flocks of birds that I paused to gaze at as they flew north overhead or as they congregated in fields or in the marshes. I finally arrived in Havre and I sold out in maybe an hour or two and was on my way home by noon. As I drove back south it started to cloud up a little. A few minutes more and it started to rain, so I rolled up the windows. Another half an hour and it was starting to get quite chilly so I put on some heat. A few minutes after that I noticed a little frozen participation on the window. I put on the defroster. Now it was snowing, a little at first, but then it really came down and it was starting to stick to the road so I had to slow down, especially since I had already taken off the snow tires. This was unbelievable as it was such a beautiful day only a few hours ago. Now it started to accumulate a few inches on the road so I pulled over at a roadside restaurant to wait out this snow squall.

I sat in the restaurant all through the afternoon and it was still snowing. I ate dinner there and finally the restaurant owner needed to close the place. There was perhaps a foot of snow on the ground now. Fortunately, there was a little motel across the street. I started my car and managed to park it in front of the motel. I checked into the motel and turned on the electric heat for about a minute before the electricity went out in the whole town. The temperature dropped like a stone and I bundled up the best I could and finally got to sleep. I woke up the next morning and looked outside and it was still snowing! I also could not see my car at all. Besides, I had only a windbreaker and sneakers and no gloves. I made my way through the snow which was by now about five feet deep. I knew where my car had been and finally found myself standing on the roof. The only way to get on to the street was to dig the car out with my bare hands. After about a half an hour of this I finally opened a space that I could back out and of course, a big plow came by and plowed me back in again. I repeated the same thing again.

Finally, I got my car out onto the street. I just wanted to go home, but when I got to the edge of town there was a state trooper placing a barricade blocking the road. He was only letting people pass who had 4-wheel drive vehicles as there were many snow drifts on the highway. I waited there for about an hour until he left to go to lunch. After he left I decided to drive around the barricade. There were many snowdrifts but I blasted through them at high speed and finally made it to the next town, Great Falls. The sun came out which made me feel better and everything was starting to melt. I had less than an hour to go. I just had to make it through the last mountain pass going over the divide and I would be home. The snow banks went all the way up to the telephone wires in places. As I drove towards the mountain pass I saw another state trooper in sunglasses in the middle of the road leaning against his car with a big grin. I pulled over when he motioned to me. He asked me where I thought I was going. I told him "to Missoula "and he replied, "Well, you're not going to make it to Missoula today. There's been an avalanche and there is fifty feet of snow in the mountain pass and 24 tractor trailers stuck in the snow." I asked him, "How long"? He replied, "About a week!"

Sometimes we did weekend one day workshops up in the National Bison Range. This is without a doubt one of the most spectacular spots in the entire country. From the top you can see Flathead Lake to the north and the glacier coming down towards the lake. To the east is the spectacular MacDonald Range of the Rockies that extends all the way up into Canada. Everywhere you can see big horn sheep, bison, elk and other animals. Despite the beautiful scenery, nature and all of our efforts, witnessing did not produce many results. Nevertheless, I loved Montana and it's one of my all-time favorite spots.

ON THE ROAD AGAIN.......
AND AGAIN......AND AGAIN.....

On the road again
Like a band of gypsies we go down the highway
We're the best of friends
Insisting that the world be runnin' our way
And our way is on the road again
Just can't wait to get on the road again
The life I love is makin' music with my friends
And I can't wait to get on the road again
          "On the Road" Again by Johnny Cash and Willie Nelson

OWC, the words mean International One World Crusade. When Rev. Moon began his evangelism in the United States in the early 70's, he went from state to state giving his message with a team of missionaries that would make preparations, invite people and meet with local dignitaries in the various major cities throughout the country. In 1983, when Rev. Moon reinitiated the IOWC, he formed 50 teams of twenty-five members, one in each state. I was assigned to lead the team that was forming in Boise, Idaho.

Our team consisted of members from Japan, Brazil, France, Mexico, and the United States. The Brazilians and some of the Japanese spoke absolutely no English at all. Communication was nearly impossible with the Brazilian brother. I felt so sorry for him because he was a little older and I felt he would have benefitted our team if he could have learned a little English before he came. It certainly wasn't his fault because he was asked to come here with absolutely no notice. The Japanese pretty much took care of themselves and were highly motivated.

Eventually our team worked out a way to communicate. Three of the sisters who volunteered were several months pregnant. They could not do all the activities physically, but they persevered nonetheless. I admired them greatly. When they left to give birth to their child I felt that they were indeed saints.

One day I had to drive up to Seattle from Boise to attend a meeting with the other leaders who headed up their own teams. I drove through endless miles of desert, the temperature rising to well above 100 degrees. Most vehicles back then had no air conditioning. I got quite sleepy and must have dozed off while driving in the heat. I heard a voice. It was the voice of Elvis Presley. With that deep Southern twanged voice, he said to me loudly, "Mark, wake up!" I opened my eyes in time to see the tractor trailer and turn to the left, spinning out in the desert sand.

Our IOWC team stayed for 21 days in each state and then moved to the next state. We received new vans from National Headquarters and eventually a couple of motor homes. Still, this lifestyle was very harsh and we often lived in cramped quarters, jamming 25 people into small homes or apartments. The driving was endless. That year I figured that I drove over 100,000 miles. I once drove for 29 hours straight from Missoula, Montana to Minneapolis, Minnesota, stopping in Yellowstone for a little side trip. We visited Portland, Seattle, Missoula, Minneapolis, Fargo, Sioux Falls, Des Moines, Milwaukee, Chicago, St. Louis, Louisville and finally Detroit, spending 3 weeks in each place.

The Upper Midwest in winter is amazingly cold. Sometimes we had to keep our cars running all night long. I took some members on a fundraising trip through parts of Nebraska and South Dakota. It was so bitterly cold but none of them complained. We got stranded in a little town after a blizzard and stayed in motel rooms that were like an ice chest even with the electric heat on full. In the morning the temperature had gone down to minus 40. No one's car would start. I called the only garage in town to have us towed into a garage to warm up the vehicle and was told it would be a 3 day wait. No way could I do that with 8 or 9 people. There was an old man going around door to door starting people's cars for 10 bucks. All he used was a Maxwell House Coffee can, a 2 gallon can of gasoline and a rag. I saw him put about an inch of gasoline in the can, place the can under the engine block of some guy's car, stick the rag in and light it up, running away quickly. Voom! The car was enveloped in flames for about 5 seconds and the flames went out. The owner got into the car and it started right up! I said a prayer and gave the old man ten bucks. It worked!

In every town we did rallies and invited guests to dinners and church sponsored events. Sometimes we had good attendance, sometimes not. Altogether we got five new members that joined, but none of them stayed for very long. Working that hard for no result was very difficult for me to deal with. Fortunately, I found a good friend, Reiner Vincenz. Reiner headed up an IOWC team as well. He was one of the first members to join from Europe. He was also the first missionary for the Unification Church in France and had worked with Ursula in Germany and England. He called me "Marcus Hendlein" to remind me that I was now part of the Fatherland and should claim my adopted German heritage. He and I would talk about church matters for many hours at a time. We often wondered how all the members could continue with this under such difficult and frustrating circumstances. The conclusion we came to was that the real question of this activity was not how many new members we would gain but how many we would have left. We began to realize that this course was like Moses' course. In other words, we were wandering in the desert until we would come into the land of Canaan. It was very difficult to understand much less persevere, but we continued this way for almost a year, surviving by faith alone.

I respect all my team members that continued with me through Detroit when we finally ended IOWC. I don't think I was able to inspire them very much. When I see some of them occasionally nowadays I feel sorry that I didn't sympathize more with their difficulties. The fact that they persevered through such an ordeal is hard to comprehend. All we really had was each other and God for that entire year.

MOTOWN TO CHICAGO

So let us all go back
back to the old landmark
and we'll stay in the service of the Lord
                    "The Old Landmark" by Aretha Franklin

When IOWC was disbanded in 1984 our church was facing so many challenges. There was the court case over tax evasion that concluded with Rev. Moon serving 18 months in Danbury Federal Penitentiary. I don't want to dwell on the content of that event. Anyone who wants to study about it can read any number of books and articles on the subject. I have obviously made up my own mind about the outcome. Let me suggest "To Bigotry No Sanction" by Mose Durst and "Inquisition: The Persecution and Prosecution of the Reverend Sun Myung Moon" by Carlton Sherwood if you like legal stuff.

One of the things that happened as a result of the court case was that many people, especially clergy, viewed the court case as a witch hunt and saw Rev. Moon as a champion for religious freedom. This enabled us to reach out to churches, religious organizations and other patriotic groups that saw this case as a threat to themselves and create bonds of friendship and solidarity.

When I was appointed as State Director of Michigan in 1984 the first order of business was to create programs with those clergy who had supported us during the court case, and especially now, since Rev. Moon was incarcerated. Our IOWC team members mostly stayed in Detroit but we sent out small groups to several cities to form pioneer city centers in Lansing, Grand Rapids, Kalamazoo and Flint. We met with every member of the clergy of every known denomination not once, but many times. We sent out countless invitations to various programs. In addition, we sent Divine Principle lecture series videotapes to every single member of the clergy in the entire United States.

At this time we began to receive donations and equipment bought from funds that came largely from Japan. Each state in the country got new vehicles including 5 motor homes for street witnessing and 5 large trucks that were to be used for redistribution of surplus foods to needy communities. On top of that, we were witnessing to ministers across the state of Michigan and inviting them to interfaith functions in hotels all throughout Michigan and to other cities throughout the United States. My schedule was very demanding and I was constantly driving across the state or for meetings in Chicago or flying to New York, St. Louis or other places. All this time Rev. Moon was still in prison. The pressure to succeed in this activity was creating a lot of stress for me that was not healthy.

Fortunately, I had one good friend that I could confide in and share my struggles with. His name is Michael Jenkins. My son, Michael, is named after him. Mike Jenkins was the Regional Coordinator for the Chicago area. There is no more hard working, passionate person that I can think of. When I left Detroit to work in Chicago I was lucky enough to work with him. We mostly worked with clergy from other churches, but I was assigned to teach Divine Principle for the 7 days and 21 days workshops for several months in Western Michigan. Teaching the Principle to new guests was refreshing and being in the camp was relaxing. When you teach something to someone it makes you learn it in a different way than just studying it. I'm not sure how many new guests were reborn through my lectures, but for me, it put me back in touch with what had originally motivated me. I was able to reclaim myself and calm my spirit.

Working on the south side of Chicago was an interesting experience.

There are thousands of small and large churches on the south side. I met with many clergy while there, including Jesse Jackson. We tried to serve the community in any way we could. One way was to help redistribute surplus government foods to churches and organizations in Chicago. We started a program with a few other churches called NCCSA (National Council for Church and Social Action) which was able to access and redistribute the surplus foods. One of the things I did was to visit churches on the south and west side and introduce the program.

One day I met an elderly woman pastor named Rev. Barnes. She had a small Pentecostal church on the south side. She was very friendly and invited me in. We sat for a while in the kitchen and talked about the program. Her church building was in very bad shape and obviously needed a new roof and a paint job. She also had a disabled son living upstairs that she took care of. Her church had 7 members. I also noticed that there was a very bad gas leak in the building. I didn't want to insult her but I felt I needed to mention the gas leak. She replied, "Oh, is that what that is? Gee, I don't know how I can get that fixed. Could you fix it for me?" I felt obligated to help her so I came back that evening with some tools and repaired the leak. She was very grateful and invited me to her church service. I went a couple of times and she sometimes invited me for tea. Rev. Barnes seemed to know everyone and she helped me to meet with quite a few other clergy. Everyone seemed to know her and think highly of her. She came to some other of our ecumenical events and was a staunch supporter for many years. One day she said to me, "I'm having a birthday party for Mayor Harold Washington and I would like to invite you to come." Realizing that the mayor of Chicago is more powerful than the presidents of most nations I thought to myself, "There is no way in hell that the mayor of Chicago is coming here for his birthday party." Nevertheless, I told her I would come of course and I would bring Mike Jenkins and some people to fill up the hall. She was very excited and set out to decorate the church. She sent me to buy a birthday cake with 65 candles. Finally, the day came and I'm still thinking, "No way." There were all of 15 people in the church. But at 6:30 these two big black SUVs pulled up to the front door and several obviously armed security guards strolled into the church. Then in came this short black mayor with a very large grin, hugged everybody, shook our hands and walked up onto the stage. As he was giving his speech I noticed that reporters from the Chicago Tribune had come in the door. They snapped the picture of the mayor blowing out the candles. The photo took up half the front page of the next day's Chicago Tribune!

Later, I found out the rest of the story. You see Harold Washington grew up on the streets of Chicago. He never knew who his father was and his mother died of a drug overdose when he was 10. Rev. Barnes, then in her 20s, took him in and raised him as if he were her own son, making sure he graduated from high school. While he was mayor he called her almost every evening and he would discuss whatever he was going to do with her. So, you never know when you meet someone who they are or what kind of foundation they have in their life.

I was able to go to Korea and Japan twice with ministers from various denominations for Divine Principle seminars and sightseeing. In Japan, I visited the Meiji Jingo Shrine, the Emperor's palace and walked through several sections of Tokyo. I played pachinko (a Japanese gambling game) and lost. In Korea I visited the demilitarized zone with North Korea and went to Panmunjom. There, we saw a fake city that is portrayed as this ideal village by North Korea, but when you look at it through binoculars, you can see that even though it is beautiful, there are in fact no people living there. We saw one of the invasion tunnels that were dug under the DMZ by the North Koreans only to be discovered in the nick of time by the South. The tunnel was wide enough to drive tanks and many thousands of soldiers and pieces of equipment through. Seoul Korea is really an amazing place. We stayed in fantastic hotels in Korea and Japan like the Miyako and the Keiyo Plaza in Shinjuku. Korea and Japan are so different from the United States in many ways. Nevertheless, I felt very much at home in both countries.

We did literally hundreds of seminars in hotels in Chicago while I was there. In each seminar, we tried every way possible to teach the Divine Principle and educate them. Mike Jenkins and I and several of the Chicago members essentially lived in hotels for almost two years. We were able to bring over 10,000 clergy from the area to these 2 or 3 day seminars. His determination to reach out to at times ungrateful and arrogant clergymen of other churches was astounding.

One time, during one of the programs, a woman pastor decided to use the pool after hours while everyone else was eating dinner. There were perhaps 400 participants in the dining hall. I left briefly for an errand, and looking down into the pool from the balcony noticed the woman face down in the center of the pool. I screamed and ran downstairs, by which time someone was pulling her out of the pool. I called 911. She was not breathing. The lifeguard, who was still in the building, proceeded to give mouth to mouth resuscitation and chest pumps to no avail. After several minutes he stopped and pronounced her dead. Michael Jenkins said, "No!" with a loud voice and took over from the lifeguard who tried to assure Michael that she was in fact dead. Pushing the lifeguard aside, he continued to try to resuscitate the lifeless woman with mouth to mouth and chest pumps for several more minutes. Suddenly she vomited in his face and came back to life. It was the most incredible thing I ever saw. He was absolutely determined to save this woman. I felt that I was very lucky to have someone like this as a friend. He never gave up, even when everyone else, including the lifeguard, our church staff, myself and all 400 people had written her off.

His attitude is like that. He would go to the ends of the earth just to give someone some blessing or to help them to realize their value. His work ethic is unbelievable. When we worked to educate ministers he was on the go 24/7/365 for almost 5 years. He just never stopped. At the same time, he understood that even though all of us worked hard, we needed to experience the ideal in some form from time to time. We became a very tight group in Chicago and we were by far the most successful city for ecumenical outreach. The result of his work, and ours, is evident even today as the American Clergy Conference (ACC) is very active and has produced very supportive clergy from almost every denomination.

> *Jake: We're putting the band back together.*
> *Mr. Fabulous: Forget it. No way.*
> *Elwood: We're on a mission from God.*
>   John Belushi and Dan Ackroyd in The Blues Brothers

I worked in Chicago until 1987. I did not have an official church position for nearly two years. I guess you could say I was Mike Jenkin's assistant, but it was good not to have a title for those two years. Ursula was still working very hard in Philadelphia but we got together on occasions and wrote to each other much more often. I was looking forward to the day where we would live together. That day was quickly approaching.

Ursula, camping on MFT

RELAX, YOU'RE IN THE SOUTH NOW!

This is for all the lonely people
Thinking that life has passed them by
Don't give up until you drink from the silver cup
And ride that highway in the sky
　　　　　　"Lonely People" by Dan and Catherine Peek, America

One day Mike asked me if I would consider being state director in Dallas, Texas. I was essentially happy working in Chicago and didn't want to leave there, but the temptation of a new adventure was too great so I agreed to pack up and move to Dallas. I still could just about carry everything I owned.

The drive down to Dallas was long and I needed to get a cup of coffee to drive the last two hours. I pulled over into a "Mom and Pop" type restaurant and sat at the counter. The waitress came up to me and asked me what I would like. Now, I am a Bostonian, and I tend to talk too fast and when I'm a little tired I tend to mumble a bit.

I replied, in one syllable with a half voice, "KnIhvakupacoffepls?"

The woman came back with a heavy Texas drawl slowly with a big voice, "Naow wud you sayee?"

I repeated my one syllable "KnIhvakupacoffepls?" with head down.

She turned around to her husband, "Now wud haee sayee?"

The husband replied deliberately, "He waunts a cup of cowfee!"

The woman turned back to me angrily. "Now wa didn't you sayee so! You Yankees are all the same! You tawk too fayist. Ya mumble under your braithe. Relax, you're in the South now! I'll git you your cup of cowfee and we'll set rye cheer and you c'n tail me all about it. We'll tawk a while. Then you'll feel much better and we'll send you on your way, Okay?" Ah yup. I was definitely in the south now.

Being a state leader again felt a little uncomfortable. I didn't want to be called "Reverend", but there was no getting around it down in the Bible belt. I had a hard time dealing with the goals we were trying to accomplish. I felt that this center life, with its discipline and soldier mentality, was not helping us to move on to the next level of family life. Our church really did not make this transition well, and we lost a lot of good members along the way. I certainly didn't understand this new direction. I hung on as a center member and leader perhaps longer than anyone. Eventually, though, most of the center members did move on to create families and they left the center and started their private lives with their spouses, raising children and contributing to the church wherever they could.

When Ursula came to Texas I felt that I had literally been saved. I guess that's the way it's supposed to feel. All my former doubts and struggles seemed to vanish as balloons poked with a pin. Our first "apartment" was a motor home parked behind the center in Dallas. At this point I was no longer the state leader, but I did some church work together with Ursula. Ursula and I also worked in some temporary mall kiosks that we set up in Mesquite and in Little Rock, Arkansas.

We eventually saved up some money so that Ursula and I could go to Germany to meet her family there. With me though, as you can tell by now, nothing comes easily. There's always a price to be paid. Call it indemnity if you want to or in my case, just plain lazy stupidity. We set the dates to leave for Ursula's hometown of Esslingen, Germany. Flying

Lufthansa, we were to stay for nearly a month. Everything was all set. We bought some non-refundable tickets. We had passports, gifts, new clothes, luggage, everything.

About a week before our departure Ursula asked me if I had my passport. I said, "Sure, it's in the box where I usually keep it." Finally, the day arrived to leave. I looked in the box. It was gone, no passport, anywhere in the house. I could not find it and to this day it is still missing. I finally concluded that someone stole it and sold it on the black market. I told Ursula and she of course started to cry. I considered suicide for a fraction of a second and then suggested that perhaps we would just go to the airport and try to board the plane anyhow.

We stood in line at Lufthansa and finally spoke to the agent.

"Sir, do you have your tickets?"

"Yes"

"....and your passport?"

"No, I've lost it. I don't know where it is."

"Well sir, you're not going to be able to go."

"I know that. But, we want to go anyways."

She didn't know what to do with me, so she sent us to her boss. We went back and forth with him for a while. He didn't know what to do either so we got in touch with the American consulate in Frankfurt, Germany. We spoke with him and finally he said that he could get us on the plane but he had no guarantee that I wouldn't be turned around and sent home on the next available flight. We decided that was fair enough, so we got on the plane, not knowing what to expect when we got to Germany.

We arrived in Frankfurt. But, when we tried to go through German customs I was immediately detained in a holding cell and spent the better part of the day there. Considering the fact that I was trying to enter the country without a passport I would say I was treated well by the German authorities. Eventually I got in touch with the American consulate again and he said that he could get me into a cab that would take us directly to the U.S. Embassy and I would be issued a new passport. When we arrived at the Embassy the consulate proceeded to lecture me for 45 minutes on the dangers of terrorism, but I eventually got a new passport for a 250 dollar charge. Then this detainee was finally allowed to meet his new relatives for the first time, an embarrassing moment to say the least.

Despite our awkward beginning, however, Ursula's mother and the rest of her family, including two sisters, two brothers and their spouses treated us with great hospitality and love. I felt very much at home and at ease in all their homes. This was my first trip to Europe. Germany really is an amazing country. Spotlessly clean it is so beautifully laid out and well planned. People have great pride in the appearance of the place they call home, much more so unfortunately than we do here in the states.

I also gradually became aware of how steeped in tradition and how long this culture has existed in comparison to the USA. On the first night we walked down the street to a small restaurant for dinner. The waiter was very friendly and served us excellent dishes. As we were eating I noticed the unique European architecture of the place. I especially noticed the huge wooden beams that held up the ceiling. They very old and had obviously been hand hewn. I wondered how old the restaurant was and mentioned it to Mrs. Arndt. When the waiter came by again they asked him and he replied off handedly in German, "I'm not sure but it's been in my family since 1192!" The number took a while to sink in. Later we went to a church built by Charlemagne! (That's 800 AD.). The next day we walked the beautiful cobblestone streets of downtown Esslingen and Ursula commented that the cobblestones were part of the Appian Way, built by the Romans.

I noticed that all the houses and apartments wherever I went had beautiful, meticulously cared for flower boxes that hung below every window of every home and apartment. They were so colorful with each one different yet perfectly placed and pruned to perfection. After a few weeks I wondered how on earth could every person in the country be persuaded to create such a national display, so I asked my mother in-law about it. I told her that in America people could never be persuaded to do this. She told me that in Germany there is a flower box ordinance. There are flower box police. If one does not keep his/her flower box up to snuff they are issued a fine. I told her that in America, unfortunately, people would not agree to such a rule.

Southern Germany near the Swiss and French borders is the home of bell towers, grandfather clocks and cuckoo clocks. No matter where you go it is "ding dong," "bing bong" or "cuckoo, cuckoo," 24 hours a day, 7 days a week. There was a large bell tower less than 100 feet from Ursula's home. It rang loudly every 15 minutes all through the night. I found it very difficult to sleep as I was constantly awoken by the bells, yet I seemed to be the only one bothered by it. When I asked Ursula about it she said that when she first came to America she found it very hard to sleep. Eventually she realized it was because there was no sound of the bells during the night. I eventually did get used to it and it didn't bother me at all.

In Germany, there is pretty much a castle on every corner. We visited a few, including the famous Hohenzollern Castle, center of many historical battles in German history. It was the ancestral home of German Kings since the 11ᵗʰ century. It contains items from German history as well as a letter from George Washington thanking Baron von Stueben for his service in the American Revolutionary war.

It really was a great trip. When we left I felt such a closeness to her mom and all her relatives. Even though we seldom meet them they are so supporting and loving people. I wondered if they would accept me since our religious beliefs were so different, but with them it has never been an issue. Their attitude has always been sincere and loving towards both Ursula and myself.

Our first "house" was the former city center in San Antonio, Texas. One of my favorite cities, San Antonio is large but very laid back with a large Hispanic population. A year after we arrived in San Antonio all US members were asked to serve for 40 days as missionaries in foreign countries. I was assigned to Dahomey, more commonly known as Benin, a very small country in West Africa between Togo and Nigeria. I sent away for and received visas to Benin and Ivory Coast. The only way to get to Benin in 1991 was by train from Ivory Coast. Ursula and I raised the nearly 2000 dollars for me to make the trip. I was just about ready to book a ticket when I was asked if I wanted to go to the Soviet Union instead. I saw this as a unique opportunity. Ever since I was a child I wondered about life behind the Iron Curtain. Ursula's parents had escaped from East Germany in the 1950's just before the erection of the Berlin Wall. All her other relatives remained in the Communist sector.

As our plane left Helsinki, Finland for the final leg to Tallinn, Estonia we only had a few minutes to complete the paperwork to enter the Soviet Union. I was less concerned about the paperwork than to look out the window and see the Baltic Sea and the coast of the Baltic Republics. I finished the paperwork just as the plane landed. As the plane docked at the gate a single soldier with a Kalashnikov rifle entered the plane. Yep, we were in the Soviet Union. As we went through the line submitting our paperwork, I was roughly pulled aside into another area and then asked to explain about my paperwork. It seemed I had made a terrible mistake in my paperwork. I wrote out the year of my birth using standard numbers rather than the words "nineteen hundred fifty-three." The government agent proceeded to dress me down in perfect English, demeaning me because I didn't follow the instructions correctly in my own language. I felt like telling him to get a life but decided that would probably not be wise. Welcome to the Soviet Union, the Union of Soviet Socialist Republics.

We proceeded out of the airport to catch our "ride." We had arranged with the Ministry of Education to have an interpreter meet us at the airport and drive us for an hour or so to the school in Latvia where we were going to teach. There were three of us on the curb waiting to be picked up. All of the other passengers boarded a bus headed for downtown Tallinn. There were literally no other vehicles at the airport except for an ambulance with a driver who was taking a nap. We waited for quite a while. Eventually we started to worry. Here we were in a communist country, the wrong country at that, and we couldn't speak the language. Suddenly, the driver of the ambulance woke up, and spotting us, realized we were the ones he was supposed to pick up. We realized we were going to get a ride in an ambulance. He was very friendly and greeted us warmly and opened up the back of the ambulance. It really was an ambulance and had all the emergency equipment in it. It also had a large pile of potatoes in the back. We threw our luggage on top of the potatoes and hopped in.

"So, this is a real ambulance?"

"Yes, this a real ambulance."

"You're an ambulance driver?"

"Yes, I'm an ambulance driver."

"OK. What's up with the potatoes?"

"Well, you know this is the Soviet Union. People only make 12 dollars a month. So, everybody sells something on the side. So, while I'm waiting for a call I set up on the side of the road and when I get a call I cover up the potatoes and come back later."

We saw so many unexpected things in the Soviet Union. When we got to the school near Daugavpils, Latvia., there were a few days we got to spend just getting acclimated. In the evenings we would walk through the village and mingle with the locals. Latvia is like the land of the midnight sun in late June. The sun just dips below the horizon and comes right back up. The days are warm and the nights are comfortable and cool. This was a very rural area. In the evening people would be out in the fields cutting hay by hand and putting it in horse drawn carts, just like they did in the middle ages. At the same time, Mig fighter jets would scream overhead at Mach 2, shattering the quiet of the evening, just to intimidate the people. One of my associates was Daryl Clarke, an African American. The townspeople had never seen a black person. Daryl is about 6'2" and powerfully built. He is also exceptionally dark, something like a shorter version of Shaquille O'Neil. Once, we went into a store and stood in line. An elderly woman turned around and saw him and almost fainted. Then a little boy came up to him and tried to rub the darkness off his skin.

We became instant celebrities in the town. Every night we went for a walk through the quaint little village. It became very comfortable to be there. One evening we saw many people out cutting hay as usual, but amongst them was a group of eight or ten young girls, perhaps 16 or 17 years old. They were cutting hay just like everyone else, but they were dressed up in traditional costumes, hoop skirts and white blouses with ruffled sleeves. They were there several nights consecutively. Finally, I asked the interpreter why these girls were dressed up like this. He looked at me angrily. "Don't you get it? These girls are doing this for your benefit! This is the Soviet Union! They want to leave! They want to go to the US of A and eat McDonald's hamburgers and drive around in Chevrolets. They are hoping that one of you handsome young guys will bring one of them back with you when you go!" At that moment I felt foolish and embarrassed. We asked him to please tell the young ladies that they are really very beautiful and that if we were not already happily married that we would be happy to take one of them home with us. Needless to say, they no longer dressed up in the evenings.

Once, I was walking through downtown Vilnius in Lithuania. There were so few stores open in the huge city. However, I did come across one duty free store that had handmade accordions and violins hanging from the window. Of course, I went in to check it out. There was a craftsman in the store making an accordion. I tried one of them. It was an exquisite machine, with mother of pearl, all handmade components. This magnificent instrument came with a handmade plush case. I had worked in music stores and I estimated in the United States the accordion would cost from 1200 to 2000 dollars. I asked him how much the instrument cost. His response was, "Ten dollars." I laughed and then, realizing that was really the price said that I would take it. The man put the 2000 dollar accordion into the plush case. I tried to hand him the ten bucks but he proceeded to hand me a receipt and pointed to a small bullet proof glass booth with a cranky looking woman in government attire inside. I handed her the receipt and the ten bucks. She stamped the receipt and gave it back to me. I handed the receipt to the craftsman and walked out of the store, bewildered at my good fortune. Though I now had a very cool souvenir to take back home, as I walked along I was very bothered by what I had just experienced. I had just paid 10 dollars for this 2000 dollar instrument that this amazing craftsman had built by hand, taking perhaps three weeks to build. Not only that, but the poor man didn't even get the ten bucks! The money had gone to the government! I lugged this instrument around for a few weeks, but in the end, I donated it to a school. To me, taking it home would have felt like I was stealing it.

Oh, God, my Father, give me light to carry o'er this earth;
For if I cannot help this world, then what is my life worth?
To help your precious kingdom come gives meaning to my birth.
Precious light warm and bright.

From "Precious Light" by Jon Schuhart

In the little more than two months we were there we taught the Divine Principle to several thousand students from all over the Soviet Union. But it was leaving the country that was the most amazing, unexpected thing. For many years I had put in a lot of time working with people who were dedicated to the eradication of the theory of Communism and providing a counterproposal. People that I worked with included former Black Panther Eldridge Cleaver, Anthony Bryant and others, some who had given their lives for that cause. One of my friends, Lee Shapiro, a journalist, was killed by the Soviets in Afghanistan trying to document the plight of the Afghan freedom fighters in that country. In reflection, it couldn't have been a coincidence that we were there precisely at the moment when the Communist system came crashing down.

Students in USSR seminar, 1991. Some of them were the
first to hear the Divine Principle from their countries.

The day we were set to leave Latvia was August 19th, 1991. We needed
to catch a train from Riga to Moscow because Moscow was the only place
you could leave the USSR from. As we boarded the bus from Daugavpils
to Riga, someone mentioned to me that Mikhail Gorbachev, the president
of the Soviet Union, had been arrested and taken captive by the hard line
Communists and military. They had declared martial law. I wasn't sure
what that meant but when we got to the train station in the center of town
there was an angry mob starting to form in the town square which is right
where the train station is. At one point I estimated there were perhaps
10,000 people there protesting the establishment of martial law. Just then
we saw a long line of Russian tanks, troop transports and foot soldiers
coming straight up the road toward the center of town. Helicopter gunships
circled the train station. The helicopters trained their large caliber guns
on the crowd, and us! Just then we were able to board the train. The train
left the station, just as the Soviet army entered the square to disperse the
protesters. I later found out that there were 8 people killed in that conflict.

Now we were on the train to Moscow, an exhilarating ride through the
countryside normally, but we didn't know what to expect when we arrived

in Moscow 16 hours later. When the train pulled into Moscow there were military vehicles everywhere. The airport was closed and being guarded by 500 tanks. There was no way we could leave at that point. However, we were able to find someone that we knew who had an apartment downtown. He agreed to put us up for a few days. We watched the unfolding events on CNN and walked around Moscow. There were several violent confrontations that we did not witness but came upon the scene of just a few hours afterwards.

We did a little sightseeing in Moscow, but everyone in the city was totally preoccupied with the political situation. Everywhere we went, people were reading handbills or watching TV monitors. We got a little hungry for lunch. Russian food was horrible and we wanted anything different after two and a half months of borsht and kvass. We came upon a Korean sign, obviously a Korean restaurant. I just love Korean food. We went in and we could smell the bulgogi and kim chee. It was like a bit of heaven. We ordered. It was just us few Americans in there and the Korean staff. I turned around and there was a picture of Kim Il Sung on the wall! This place was a North Korean establishment! Just then, about 20 mean looking North Korean soldiers dressed in green uniforms came in! They sat all around us. They ordered and as they talked they kept looking over our way. After a while I could hear "Mi gooki, Mi gooki," which in Korean means "Americans, Americans." This was becoming quite a tense situation. We decided to order a round of sake for the soldiers. The dollar was quite strong compared to the ruble, so it only cost maybe five dollars. They were quite surprised and happy at our gesture, so we ordered them another round of sake. Soon we were singing some Korean songs together that I knew. Teary eyed, we shook their hands and left after a great meal.

Arirang, arirang, ario
Arirang ko ge ro nomaganda
Se anu se dangi ee ryu jo ne
Se no re pu ru yo
Dang myun ha se.
Arirang, arirang, ario
We are crossing over the crest of the hill
Let us sing together with a new heart
We shall see the dawning of a great new day

"Arirang", ancient Korean folk melody

The political situation in Moscow reached a critical point when some of the Russian tank drivers broke off from their Communist comrades and formed a skirmish line in front of the Russian Federation Building in downtown. We watched on CNN (as many did in the US) as ordinary Russian citizens came to the aid of these brave soldiers. They built a huge barricade perhaps thirty feet high that encircled the Federation building. At this point we decided there was no way we could just sit and watch this on TV. We were Americans. We had to go and support these brave people in their desperate push to finally overthrow Communism and establish a free democratic state.

Tass Hdqtrs, August, 1991, information and propaganda
publishing house in the Soviet Union

When we arrived at the Federation Building we had to pass the communist tank line and a burned out bus. We scaled the barricade together with hundreds of other Russian citizens. There were already tens of thousands of people inside waving Russian flags. There were rock bands playing and passionate speeches being made. I shook hands with many of the tank drivers. A lot of people were putting flowers in the tank barrels. Some of these images you may have seen on CNN.

When you arrive in the Soviet Union, one of the first things you notice is that no one smiles. Yet, here, as Russians breathed the fresh air of freedom in their country for the first time, you could see people smiling, hugging and crying tears of hope and joy. I realized that God had allowed me to come here at this precise moment, another reminder that he is in control of our lives and that he remains the main force behind history as it pushes forward towards the establishment of his kingdom.

> *Mine eyes have seen the glory of the coming of the Lord*
> *He is trampling out the vintage where the grapes of wrath are*
> *stored,*
> *He has loosed the fateful lightning of His terrible swift sword*
> *His truth is marching on.*
> *Glory! Glory! Hallelujah!*
> *Glory! Glory! Hallelujah!*
> *Glory! Glory! Hallelujah!*
> *His truth is marching on.*
>
> "Battle Hymn of the Republic"

When I returned home I realized that the world was quite different than when I left for the Soviet Union. Communism had been defeated. We were entering the post-Cold War era. The world seemed a little friendlier. Our church was also entering a new phase. Rev. Moon was sending members worldwide back to their hometowns to raise their families and to witness. Scott McKenna, the state leader in Arkansas, was leaving for Pennsylvania soon. I was asked if I would like to try one more time at state leadership. Since Ursula and I had no children we thought that it would be a good step to try this position as a couple. We packed up and headed for Little Rock, Arkansas.

While in Arkansas, we started a business raising and selling bonsai trees. This was an excellent hobby business for a while, though it was somewhat labor intensive, repotting, pruning, watering, wiring trees and carting them around by truck. At one point, we had over 1000 small potted trees in our back yard. The movie The Karate Kid had recently come out, so bonsai was quite the rage for a few years. Unfortunately, bonsai are quite difficult to care for. It requires a lot of knowledge to make them grow and survive in small containers. Nevertheless, they made good gifts and we did pretty well for about 3 years with it.

While we were in Little Rock we were visited by Mrs. Hak Ja Han Moon, wife of Rev. Moon. She was on a speaking tour of the United States. It was a very intense time preparing and inviting people and dignitaries. We booked the best hotel in Little Rock for the event. After the speech she met for several hours with the members of Arkansas and some others from surrounding states who came to join us. It was interesting because Bill Clinton had just been elected president. Hillary Clinton wanted to use the hotel we had already had booked to have a summit for reviving the health care system, but she had to go elsewhere.

Ursula and I wished to have children, but after a while it became obvious that there was something preventing this from happening. We tried medical treatments but ran out of money and inspiration at some point. Eventually we gave up, choosing rather to focus on doing church work and maintaining the church center in Little Rock. All the members moved out of the center and some returned to their hometown. In 1993 Ursula and I decided to move back to our hometown as well.

HOMETOWN

I n the fall of 1993 Ursula and I packed all our stuff into a 1991 Hyundai and a Green Ford Ranger with a small U-Haul trailer and drove up to Manchester, New Hampshire. It was the first time I had been to New Hampshire in many years. We lived in a small apartment in Concord for a few years. My Parents had retired to Florida, my sister lived in Maine, and my brother had just moved to Houston, Texas. There were about 15 members living in the state, 40 including children. I only knew a few of the families. Ursula and I went to church on Sundays and supported the church wherever we could.

We eventually started a small retail business in the center isle of the Steeplegate Mall in Concord, NH. It was nice to have our own place in this peaceful town and just focus on family life. I applied for a few teaching jobs in the area, but since I had no recent work history it was quickly evident that it was going to take a while, if ever, to be able to work in the public school system. I did some substitute work here and there. I bought a taxi, which I drove during the off season in Concord and leased it when the mall got busy. We made some day trips up to the White Mountains and hiked a few smaller mountains and waterfalls. I met a few of my old classmates and went to my 25th High School reunion. It was great to reconnect to my former stomping ground. I even played a few rounds of golf at Green Meadow Golf Course in Hudson, where I had worked back in the day. Ursula and I were putting some money away to buy a house. I would have been happy just to have continued this way up until now, but that's not the way God works. My life has always been full of unexpected things. Nothing is ever as simple as it seems, at least not for me.

Around this time the former state director of the church resigned and took a position in Latvia. I volunteered to fill the position but only on a part time basis. I did not want to live in the church center in Manchester, preferring to stay in our own apartment in Concord. Eventually, we sold the church building as it really was not a good place for public meetings. On Sundays we met in some of the homes of the members who lived locally. New Hampshire has some excellent and capable members living there.

The summer camp for Unificationist children is called Camp Aurora. It has been one of the best church camps in the country over the years. I have been the music director there since 1995. It is held at Geneva Point on Lake Winnipesaukee, one of the most beautiful spots in the state. The high point of my year, for 25 years now, has always been to take a week off work and go up to Camp Aurora.

Ursula and I had tried for so many years to have children. We resigned ourselves to the fact that we would remain childless. This is a difficult course to accept for people who value family above all else. Those who have children have no idea what it's like for couples in that kind of situation. Those couples who have children gravitate to others who have them. Their lives revolve around them after all. Ursula and I felt like we really didn't fit in after a while. People would stop talking (presumably about their children) when we would come into a room. We would not be invited to family type functions. On top of that, Ursula and I became very critical of other parents. To us it was easy to see how ungrateful these parents were and how they were not doing a good job. Of course, now we are making all the same mistakes other parents make. At any rate, I suppose the good thing that came through all these years was that Ursula and I got a clear opinion of what a parent should be. For a while, though, it seemed that we were being prepared for nothing.

In the fall of 1997 we moved to Manchester to be closer to the mall that we had set up our business in. It was a slightly larger apartment than what we previously had. Shortly thereafter we heard about a Korean spiritualist, a Lady Dr. Kim, who was coming to Boston and who had some ability to help couples such as ourselves to conceive through a special prayer and grace. We went along with a few other couples in a similar situation. Lady Dr. Kim supposedly had abilities to help people with other types of problems as well. We came to the meeting and fulfilled our part of the ceremony and prayer but we decided not to get our hopes up. There was one other thing that may have helped.

CANCELLING OUR MATERNITY HEALTH INSURANCE BINDER

> *You've gotta have heart*
> *All you really need is heart*
> *When the odds are sayin' you'll never win*
> *That's when the grin should start*
>
> *You've gotta have hope*
> *Mustn't sit around and mope*
> *Nothin's half as bad as it may appear*
> *Wait'll next year and hope*
>   "Heart" from the Broadway musical, "Damn Yankees"

t any rate, about two or three weeks after we decided to cancel it I came home from work one day and Ursula said,
"Hey, did you see that thing in the bathroom?"
"No, what is it?"
"It's a pregnancy tester!"

"Ok, whose is it?"

"It's yours of course!"

"Ok, what's it say? It must be wrong. Check it again."

"I've already checked it three times."

It took a few minutes to really sink in. I thought it was a joke but it was not. It really was a miracle after all that we had been through. Even now, thinking about it I am in awe of the event. Michael William Hanlon, born October 31st, 1998. In my life it has been a rule somehow to be tested until the end. Such was the case in the birth of our son as well. We went along with the program proscribed by the hospital but we decided not to have an amniocentesis as this invasive procedure presents some risk to the life of the child. We decided that the pregnancy itself was such a miracle that we in no way wanted to roll the dice on the off chance that our child would be born with some defect. We did go ahead with the Lemans course, a totally useless activity, one that seemed totally out of touch and irrelevant to the process of labor. At least that's the way I observed it. You see, doctors and nurses really have this thing figured out.

It has always been the case that God somehow sends the right person at just the right moment to receive his blessing. Childbirth seemed to be no exception to the rule. After being active the entire day Ursula went into labor at 11 pm. On top of that she was in labor for 18 hours. All that time there were different shifts of the kindest, most caring nurses that one could expect. They took care of everything that could be expected within reason with such a friendly warm attitude, explaining everything and getting all the proper items be it pillows or painkillers. However, after 18 hours, nothing was happening. Something needed to be done.

It was then that another type of nurse came on duty. She was German, just like my wife, except unlike my kind, usually soft spoken Ursula, this woman was your prototypical German nurse. Gruff, tough and take charge, she was the boss. She took one look at my wife and said, "Ursula, we got to kick zees baby out right now! No more free rides, no more free lunches!" She took one look at me. "You can leave. Go out in zee hallvay. Come back in five minutes."

I bought myself a coffee from the machine and noticed my hands shaking considerably, unable to hold it steady. In a few minutes the nurse stuck her head out the door. "Kommen zee. Your child vil be born in a couple minutes." After I cut the umbilical cord the nurse handed me this small child with a few very blond hairs. She suggested I sing him a song.

> *Oh give me a home where the buffalo roam*
> *and the deer and the antelope play.*
> *Where seldom is heard a discouraging word*
> *and the skies are not cloudy all day*
>
> *Home, Home on the range*
> *Where the deer and the antelope play*
> *Where seldom is heard a discouraging word*
> *and the skies are not cloudy all day*
>
> "Home on the Range" by Brewster M. Higley

Eleven thousand dollars; This was exactly our savings to put down on a new house. Oh well. God's plan is always different somehow from my plan. Here I was, nearly 50 years old, pushing a small child through the park in a baby stroller. "Oh, your grandson is so cute", was the popular expression.

Nothing changes your life more than having a child. My life, as I had known it was over. My focus was now only one thing; everything else was irrelevant.

Mikey in Florida visiting his grandparents

Unfortunately, our business in the mall was falling off some and Ursula was now a stay at home mom. I have essentially worked two jobs ever since. We have never taken a vacation. That's just the way it is. I'm not unhappy about it. On the contrary, our life has been infinitely enriched and purposeful. Every day is a joy. Well, almost every day.

A few months after Michael (can't call him Mikey anymore) was born I was suffering from severe occasional stomach pains, something that I had endured occasionally for about 10 years and attributed to eating something that I probably shouldn't have. I eventually got it checked out and had my gallbladder out. This procedure was botched by the surgeon and I needed an additional procedure after I nearly died from bile poisoning. I realized how fleeting life is. Grateful to still be alive, I continued with our mall business and part time cab driving. Our mall business finally went belly up and I was in the process of seeking a new career. I was able to find a part time job teaching music at a small school for performing arts in Derry. I got a few students to start and eventually had 40 students.

At the same time, I was the acting state director of the Unification Church of New Hampshire, though my activities were on a part time basis. I gave Sunday sermons, attended regional meetings, and tried to reach out to families in the area. Occasionally, we did outreach to clergy from various denominations.

Late in 2000 we heard that Rev. Moon was to make a speaking tour to every state in the United States, perhaps his last set of public appearances in the country. In New Hampshire we had maybe 10 families. This speech would require massive investments of manpower and money, neither of which we had in abundance. As state leader, I was suddenly the center of this huge mobilization. At the same time, our family was now living on credit cards. I sold my cab and decided to work exclusively for the campaign. Our small apartment became command central for this mobilization activity. We lived between charts, telephones, computer mail outs, phone lists and people in our 900 square foot apartment for nearly two months. Each state also sent people to New Hampshire to help in this campaign. We visited mayors of cities, and every church and clergyman in the state more than once to hand deliver the invitations. We invited professors of religion, army chaplains, American Legion commanders, retired military officers, newspaper and television stations and anyone we met on the street, door to door and shops in every city in the Granite State, from Portsmouth to Keene to Pittsburg.

Finally, the day of the event came. 500 people filled the Marriott Hotel in Nashua, NH. After the speech Ursula and I presented Rev. and Mrs. Moon a plaque of the State of New Hampshire featuring the Old Man of the Mountain. The members in New Hampshire and from around the region had sacrificed a lot for this event. I felt sorry that we couldn't have brought more people, but we did fill the hall and it certainly was a relief that the event was now over and we could move on to other things.

Mark and Ursula presenting Rev. and Mrs. Moon New Hampshire gift of "The Old Man of the Mountain"

Bankruptcy is a difficult thing to deal with. It makes you feel like you are worthless. I could see how such a thing can destroy families. It brings so much stress into your life. Having to go through it was an inevitable consequence of what transpired, as I described. Yet, if I had to do it all over again, I am sure that I would. There really is a silver lining in every cloud.

I was enjoying teaching privately in Derry. My guitar playing was improving and I had my clarinet overhauled as I was giving lessons now on clarinet, sax and a few other instruments. I got a second job working for a transportation company in Salem, NH driving people back and forth from Logan Airport. One day, I saw an ad for a music teaching position at a small K-12 school in northern New Hampshire. The town, Pittsburg,

NH is way up on the Canadian border, above the White Mountains. Ursula and I loved the White Mountains area. I had only been north of the White Mountains one time, but that whole area is so beautiful and pristine. I thought that I could at least go up for the interview and then decide. This was early August of 2002. It was a beautiful day, 70 degrees, blue sky, lakes, rivers, mountains. It was a beautiful school with a huge yard that sits right on the Connecticut River.

FLATLANDER

et me tell you about Pittsburg, NH, population 900, give or take. At 291 square miles it is the largest town area wise in New England. It is a snowmobile mecca and a paradise for hunters, fishermen and nature lovers. It is also a town where everyone knows everyone else, and everyone else's business. It's something like "Mayberry, RFD." As a teacher, it was like living in a goldfish bowl. Nevertheless, people are friendly, resourceful and helpful to others in need. The first year we lived there our basement got flooded and many people whom I had never met came over to help us out. It's a town where when you pass someone on the road they wave to you and then you wave back. And you'd better wave, because if you don't wave there will be consequences. What would happen is I would get a phone call from someone. "Hey, Mr. Hanlon, you didn't wave to me on the road today. Are you alright?", or a rumor would pass around about you like "Oh, Mr. Hanlon didn't wave to me on the road today. He's probably having trouble at home." Then that would go all over town until it finally got back to me.

Anyways, I went up for the interview. I had no idea what small town life was like. The superintendent said that he would send me a contract in the mail. I walked out feeling very good. I called Ursula and told her the good news and that I was going across the street from the school to get a bite to eat at the local diner.

Now I had never been in this town before in my life. I had just been interviewed 60 seconds before, walked across the street to the diner, sat at the counter, the waitress came up to me and said "Oh, you must be the new music teacher."

I was so shocked I didn't know what to say except, "Excuse me?"

"Yes, and we heard that you're going to be living in the old Washburn house."

"That's nice. Uh, who told you that?"

"Yeah, and you've got a young son. He's four years old. When he gets old enough to go to school, he could walk to school from theya. It'd be perfect!"

I later found out that this waitress was one of the best friends of the school secretary and that while I was still interviewing they were talking on the phone. So, they had my whole life planned out before I even walked out the front door.

Pittsburg really is a unique place. It was at one time an independent country. In 1832 it was known as the Republic of Indian Stream. In many ways it still is. I was called flatlander until the day I left. People not from Pittsburg are from "down below." It is a very unique and picturesque area, many mountains and streams. The headwaters of the Connecticut River are at the Canadian border. Beginning at only a few feet wide it meanders for more than 40 miles southward through the center of town, creating several lakes that are dammed at one end. It is a magnificent fishing and hunting area. The wildlife is spectacular. On any given day you have to try hard not to see a deer, moose, bear or other creature. We lived on a street known as Moose Alley, which is well known as a place to view moose in their native habitat.

When I arrived in 2002 until I left in 2012 there was no cell phone service, high speed internet, or cable television. Radio stations are essentially all in French, mostly from Canada. The nearest bank, hospital, grocery store or Dunkin' Donuts is 17 miles away. The nearest Walmart is a two hour drive, a treacherous one at that on the week before Christmas. An emergency vehicle requires 40 minutes or more to reach you if the need arises. Pittsburg has one police car with one full time officer.

The average snowfall in most of Pittsburg is more than 200 inches per year. It is the snowmobile capital of New England. On a weekend in January there might be 5,000 sleds on the 1000 miles of trails in Pittsburg. Nevertheless, we essentially never had snow days in school unless ice made the roads impassable. We hired someone to plow the driveway, but many times some unknown plow driver would just plow it for us out of the kindness of his heart.

Some of the people of Pittsburg are remarkable in their determination to maintain a simple, healthy, hard working lifestyle. When we first moved into the old Washburn house we were thrilled to see that the house had a beautiful fireplace and a wood stove in the basement. It had an older oil furnace but we decided to burn wood because it was cheaper and besides, there was already 2 ½ cords of wood stacked in the basement. Being a typical flatlander, I looked at the room full of wood and thought "Wow, that will last us the whole winter." It didn't take long to realize that I knew nothing about this lifestyle. Around mid-December I realized that we were going to run out of wood within the next month or so.

I had a neighbor, an eighty-year-old man, whom I saw constantly chopping wood in his front yard using an axe, stacking it up neatly in row after row along the street. He had a mountain of wood in the back. I called him up one evening.

"Gordon, I'm running low on wood. Could you sell me some wood?"

"Sure, how much do you need?"

"Could you sell me half a cord to get started?"

"Sure, I'll be right over."

"Wait a minute, Gordon. It's dark out. It's 20 below zero. The wind's blowing 50 miles an hour. It's blowing the snow all over the place. It's like the North Pole out there. I'll be alright for a while. Wait for a better day." The old man chirped back, "It's not getting any better. I'll be right over."

An hour later he was throwing the wood down off the back of his truck into our basement. Picture this spry wiry man. He had on a green and black checked flannel hunting shirt, a baseball hat and some thin 99 cent gardening gloves, blue jeans and work shoes. That's it. It's so cold that when you open the door it creates a cloud of steam and the cold just takes your breath away. My wife looked out the window.

"Mark, look at that poor old man out there. You gotta go out and help him." "Alright."

So, I put on my thermals, ski pants, parka with my rabbit skin hat, scarf, insulated gloves and boots. Barely able to move in all this stuff, I managed to somehow pull myself up onto the back of his pickup. I was already quite cold but I was throwing the wood down. I quickly realized that he was throwing 3 pieces to my one and I was just getting in his way.

"Gordon, look I'm cold, I'm just getting in your way. I'm going back inside. Would you like a cup of coffee?"

"No, thank you".

For ten years Gordon sold us wood, sometimes as many as nine cords that he, himself, cut by hand, just like Abe Lincoln. He would cut the pieces with a chain saw, but he would split each piece with an axe. Most of it he would sell to neighbors and relatives or keep for himself.

I asked him, "Gordon, how much wood do you cut every year?"

"Well, I don't cut as much as I usedta! Mebee fifty or sixty cord."

"Ok. How much did you use to cut?"

"Well, when I was forty or fifty, I would cut three hundred cord."

One time he came over to my house.

"Mark, this cord of wood here almost got me kilt!"

"Gordon, what happened?"

"Well I was cutting some wood offa Hall Stream and I hit a stump. I didn't know there was a bear under it asleep. Woke him up. He was none too happy, chased me into ma truck."

Then he showed me the scratches on the side of his truck. I drove up to Pittsburg last year to visit and he's still out there cutting wood, now in his mid-nineties. He does that and collects sap from sugar maples in the spring, boiling it into maple syrup. He is also the town tax collector.

Although Pittsburg is an isolated, somewhat desolate place, in an ideal world it is a model of what a village in the Kingdom of Heaven could be. I got to interact with nearly every person in the town on a regular basis. Many people serve multiple roles. As a music teacher I got to see all the good and bad. Living there for ten years was such a great opportunity. Relationships take on a whole new meaning when you have to see the same people over and over again. There were pretty much no secrets that the town didn't know.

I came to school one Monday morning and a very small first grade boy tugged on my sleeve.

"Hey, Mr. Hanlon, you had some visitors from Massachusetts over the weekend?"

"Well, how did you know that?"

"My mommy said you had a car in your driveway with a Massachusetts license plate."

That evening the woman who writes for the local weekly newspaper called me up. "Hey, Mr. Hanlon. We heard you had some visitors from Massachusetts over the weekend. We're wondering if you took them around town. Did they have a good time? Would you mind telling about it so I could put their story in the paper this week?"

I had lived for 25 years as an evangelist, but in this town, I knew right away that the most important thing to do was to witness by example. I saw the difficulties that families faced. Those who were involved with the school or in the social structure could find purpose in life. Most of them are creative, hardworking and responsible. Everyone is active in the politics of the town. Town meetings, especially those concerning the school, bring out the passions of all townspeople. You could see that everyone cared about their hometown and wanted the best for it.

Entertaining yourself is easier than you might think in a small town like Pittsburg. If you get bored in the evening, you can always take a drive up to Moose Alley and do some moose watching and get an ice cream on the way home at Moose Alley Cones. There are many great walks, our favorite being the path across the top of Murphy Dam. There was also a covered bridge across the street from our house and a beautiful path along the Connecticut River. In the summer we could ride our bikes around the village and through the school parking lot.

I tried as hard as I could to be a good music teacher and maintain my family at the same time. I can only say that in the ten years at the Pittsburg School I received an abundance of support from students and coworkers at the school. Our family kept our affiliation to ourselves. We chose to try to serve the community, and teach only by example. We faced many hardships as a family while in Pittsburg. The teacher's salary was not enough to live on, really. I eventually got a second job working in the service department of the Balsams Grand Resort Hotel in Dixville Notch.

There is a book called "1000 Places You Should Visit Before You Die." The Balsams Hotel is number 334 in the book. This place is on the National Historic Register and is the 2nd oldest resort hotel in the country.

Appearing out of nowhere as you pass Dixville Notch along Rte. 26, you feel like you just entered Switzerland. It is truly one of the most beautiful spots on earth. I worked there nights, weekends and vacations as a bellman/doorman. It was the most fun job I ever had. There is a culinary school at the hotel which is part of the Culinary Institute of America. One of my jobs there was to eat lunch or dinner there, testing the five-star dishes. It was a tough job, but someone had to do it.

The grounds of the Balsams are spectacular. The hotel is essentially the only building in the town of Dixville Notch, an area of more than 10,000 acres. The architecture is spectacular. In the summer there are 30,000 flower plants in the gardens surrounding the hotel. The hotel has accommodated many presidents and presidential candidates.

The hotel really is quite famous. It is the place where the first votes in the Presidential Election are cast and counted every four years. In the "Ballot Room" the 17 voters in Dixville Notch cast their vote at midnight and they are counted and broadcast a minute later to the world on national television. On those days media from all over the world descend upon Dixville Notch.

I even got to hang out there with a few old music buddies of mine from UMass Lowell who played in the hotel band. I played in the lobby there a few times and once at a New Year's Eve party.

As music teacher I was responsible for band, chorus, general music classes in elementary school and music theater. I never did music theater in college, but this was by far the most rewarding program. It brought together kids who had different talents and gave everyone something of value to contribute. Those who were involved in the music theater program became very close knit. Even though the work was astronomical and way beyond normal school hours, by the time the production was ready the feeling of comradery was so high that all the members of the staff, crew and players were essentially like a family. The development of skills was far more than what one might expect from a small school. You never know what kids can do. You never can assume anything about anyone.

Pittsburg School, where I taught music for 10 years

There was one student I had all through elementary. His name was Logan. He was a big friendly kid, but in elementary school he was essentially the class clown, constantly doing things inappropriate and distracting the class. He could not sit still. His parents and grandparents were big supporters of the music program, but when Logan graduated from 8th grade I was happy that I no longer had him in general music. By then he no longer sang in concerts. Most of the time he just fooled around anyways. He had tried to play the drums for a while, but this didn't work out for him either. Logan was more interested in basketball and baseball.

A few years later the high school was doing a very challenging play called Aida, a musical adapted from the Verdi opera by Elton John and Tim Rice. It's a fantastic story about the timelessness of true love, set in ancient Egypt. The excellent theme, together with the reggae, jazz, gospel, and rock and roll made it my favorite of all time. The musical score is very catchy yet challenging. One of the gospel numbers had 9 separate parts to it. The only problem I had was that I needed to fill a role that required a very high tenor part. I had no one who could even come close to hitting the high notes. I had consigned myself to having to write out the part in a lower key, not an easy assignment. It was not going to sound the same, but I felt I had no choice.

One day a female student, Danielle, came up to me and said, "Logan wants to try out for the role of Mereb."

I laughed, "No way."

"Come on Mr. Hanlon. You got to give him a chance".

"No, he's just pulling your leg. He's not serious."

"No, Mr. Hanlon. You don't understand. He can really sing".

"No way. I'm just setting myself up to be embarrassed".

"Please, Mr. Hanlon, I promise you. You won't regret it."

"Ahhh, alright".

I grew up in your hometown, at least began to grow
I hadn't got to my first shave before the body blow
Egyptians in the courtyard, my family in chains
You witnessed our abduction which possibly explains
How I know you
How I know you

"How I Know You" as sung by Mereb
from "Aida" by Elton John and Tim Rice

Finally, the day of auditions came. The last period of the day I walked downstairs to the auditorium/cafeteria where the auditions were to be held. The entire school came out to watch the auditions. The room was full. They had all come to hear Logan sing. By now Logan was the jock on campus. At 6 foot 5 and 250 he was the star of varsity sports at the Pittsburg School. Eventually, Logan got up to sing parts of Mereb's songs in the musical. He looked quite nervous but when he sang he filled the room with a powerful voice, easily hitting high Bb's with vibrato, excellent tone, perfect diction. I could see that many kids and teachers just had their mouths open. Some cried. After the song everyone turned around to look at me. All I could say was, "dude."

I asked him later, "Logan, what the heck. Nobody knew you could even sing at all, much less like that."

"Well, Mr. Hanlon, when I was in junior high, I didn't want to stick out. I didn't want the guys to know I like to sing."

After that we had almost every jock on campus wanting to be a part of the musical even if just to carry a sword or spear. We had more guys in the musicals than girls some years. We even had equal numbers of boys and girls in high school chorus for the Christmas Concert. Everyone wanted to be a part of it. The next year we did "The King and I" with a cast of 64. Logan was the king. My son, Michael, at this point a 6th grader, played the role of Anna's son.

> *I whistle a happy tune*
> *And every single time*
> *The happiness in the tune*
> *Convinces me that I'm not afraid*
>   "Whistle a Happy Tune" from The King and I

I got some great friends from amongst the staff members. Their support for the music program was unbelievable. Some of them put in almost as much time (maybe more) as I did helping to build sets, painting, making costumes etc. We had three amazing directors over the years who inspired and coached the actors. I did the music and some of the choreography. We also had some others who were professional dancers that did some great stuff. It really was a team or even a community effort. The whole town came out for the plays. I was eventually asked to give a talk at the New Hampshire Music Educators Allstate Convention about developing a successful music theater program.

During this time, we struggled to keep our affiliation with the church in Manchester, especially in the winter. Going south in winter you were sure to hit a snowstorm somewhere because in winter it is usually snowing either north of the White Mountains or south of them. We kept in touch with all the members but we honestly felt that God meant for us to have those ten years on our own, an experience that all in all was such a great blessing to us. I was able to fulfill my dream of teaching music in the public school. I felt like Job in the Bible, in a way. He lost everything, but in the end because of his faith he got it all back and then some.

I was also able to perform music with friends that I made in the community. For several years I played in a folk and Celtic band called The Folk Tree that played in many events in the region every year. It was a fun diversion that created lifelong friendships with several excellent musicians. We performed in Winter Warmer Concerts, local events and festivals and county fairs, at the Balsams Hotel and community programs. Sometimes, I performed solo either on clarinet or guitar/ vocal. My son, Michael was quite the singer back then, performing at the Balsams Hotel as well as in the Winter Warmer Concert Series.

Celebrating our 25th anniversary in Gloucester, Mass.

Being in such proximity to nature 24 hours a day was very good for me, even if I didn't feel like I was accomplishing much. One of our favorite spots was a small beach and promontory at First Connecticut Lake. We would be greeted by the local wild ducks and geese, which Mikey enjoyed feeding. Just sitting on a bench and meditating for an hour or two with no particular goal or plan, we would take in the view and listen to the call of the loons. Loons are very large, spectacularly colored water fowl. Majestic swimmers with amazing speed under water, they can remain submerged for what seems like minutes, surfacing hundreds of yards away from their dive point. Mikey and I would often go fishing, easily catching a trout or several bass, salmon or horned pout.

Though we would occasionally fellowship with families to the south, both Ursula and I wished to affiliate with a larger group. We realized that the Montreal Church was quite large. Having never been there we decided in 2009 that we would visit them. What we found was a vibrant, thriving community with many children our son's age. It took a little over 2 hours to get there on a good day, but we decided that it would be a good investment of time to participate and get to know some our brethren to the north. Some of them I had worked with in the states. They were very welcoming to us and over time we came to consider ourselves as Canadian members, except of course, when it came to hockey.

Mikey and I played in the band there on Sundays and he went to their summer youth camp as well as the New Hampshire camp. We went to potlucks and barbeques at some of the Canadian homes which made us feel very much at home. We learned a lot about life in Canada and the spirit of the members there. The Canadian Unification Church has had somewhat of a different history than the US. Though some of them worked in the United States on various campaigns, they chose not to adopt the American Unification Church model. The members themselves chose how to organize and direct their communities according to their own customs and lifestyle. The United States church, on the other hand, was and is always grappling with providential directions and mobilizations. Rev. Moon and his family lived in the US for many years, speaking, starting businesses and spent by far the majority of his time here. Canadians are very much vested in their activities and support one another, working in activities they see as important. I'm not saying one is better than the other; it's just a different approach. The Canadian church is very relaxed. They just love to hang out, eat, play music and of course watch professional hockey on TV. That's all my favorite stuff.

GOD BLESS THE BROKEN ROAD

> *Every long lost dream*
> *Lead me to where you are*
> *Others who broke my heart*
> *They were like northern stars*
>
> *Pointing me on my way*
> *Into your loving arms*
> *This much I know is true*
> *That God blessed the broken road that sent me straight to you*
>
> "God Bless the Broken Road" by Rascal Flatts

Most of the time that I experienced God in my life it was in an atmosphere of acceptance, love and family. Nevertheless, we know that since the time of our first human ancestors mistake, there have been countless tragedies that have created hell on earth. God lost his children, the objects of his love and blessing due to the fall. Since then God's ideal has been thwarted by those determined to do evil. Though God is a parent and desires only good for us, he has had to watch as his children have been abused and killed over and over again. There seems to be no end to the senseless behavior that adds to his misery daily. Most of the time we experience this torment vicariously by watching the evening news. Occasionally, we experience it directly.

"God Bless the Broken Road" is one of my favorite songs but it's one of those songs that can be hard for me to listen to or sing. In the summer of 2011 our family was visiting some friends in Montreal. On the way back, we heard on the radio that an 11 year old girl, Celina Cass, from Stewartstown, NH, was missing and police and fire rescue teams from all over New England were scouring the countryside, looking for some trace of her whereabouts. A few days later her body was discovered in the Connecticut River, having been brutally raped and murdered. Celina was a 5th grade student in the Stewartstown School where I taught on Tuesday and Thursday afternoons. She was a very humble and decent child, very supportive and never had a bad word to say about anyone or anything. She was an active participant in music, singing in concerts and competing in Stewartstown Idol, our version of American Idol. The murderer was not indicted until recently. At Celina's funeral all the people of the town released a balloon into the air, sending Celina up to heaven. This event shocked everyone in the community. Grief counselors advised the teachers how to handle this just as the fall semester began.

At first everything seemed fine. Classes seemed normal, including Celina's class which was now grade 6. However, one day, about 3 weeks into the school year, something happened that I will never forget. I started the class in our usual way. I had compiled a songbook over the years that included songs that children loved to sing. There were perhaps 50 songs in the book. Every class we would start by singing 3 songs from the book. One student suggested, "Let's sing "God Bless the Broken Road" by Rascal Flatts."

I said, "That's a pretty sad song. Are you sure you want to sing that song?" "Yeah, come on Mr. Hanlon. We love that song. Let's sing it."

"Ok, ok."

Now I can sing /play that song pretty well, maybe not as well as Rascal Flatts, but close enough. Well, we got into the first chorus of it and that boy started to cry. Another couple of bars and the whole class was in tears that would not stop for the rest of the day. You see this was Celina's favorite song. They could only tell me how much they missed Celina. Such is the power of music. It was this song that let them finally express what was pent up in them for 2 months. Later I went back to my office and was clearing out some old stuff and I noticed Celina's songbook from the year before. On the cover were many multicolored balloons that she had painted as a decoration for it.

All good things must come to an end, so they say. In 2002, when we arrived in Pittsburg, the north country of New Hampshire had three large employers that were the economic engines of the area. The Groveton Paper Mill, The Ethan Allen furniture factory and the Balsams Grand Resort Hotel employed altogether over 1000 people altogether. By 2011 all three had closed, dragging down many supporting industries with them. The Pittsburg School had lost almost 2/3 of its students. It wasn't only the music program that got cut but several teachers either lost their jobs or their positions were not replaced when they retired.

In the summer of 2012 our family moved to Worcester, Massachusetts. We chose Worcester because there is a large vibrant Unificationist community there with many children around the same age as our son. I had tried without success to find employment as a teacher in the greater Worcester area. Nevertheless, we packed up all our stuff and left for Massachusetts.

FULL CIRCLE AND BEYOND

> *And together we'll build a world that's new.*
> *That's fit for kings and fit for queens;*
> *We'll raise them up to rule the land,*
> *And place dominion in your hand.*
>
> *I'll never leave you anymore,*
> *For I have found in your bright eyes*
> *A river of love, a heart of gold,*
> *A peaceful mind, a hand to hold.*
>
> "I'll Never Leave You", Lyrics by Hillie Edwards
Music "The Water is Wide"

The last few years so many things have happened. I'm not sure I have really digested it all, so it's very difficult to write about. The founder of our church, Rev. Sun Myung Moon passed away in September 2012. His passing has had a profound effect on all Unificationists. Our church has been going through a painful transition period. His wife, Hak Ja Han

Moon, has been leading the movement for the last 4 years. Some of their children have struggled with this transition.

In late August 2012, when we learned of the imminent passing of Rev. Moon, I went for a walk with Ursula in Elm Park in Worcester. I pondered the future of our movement without this great man. As I walked I paused at a huge oak tree. The tree was very old and had many gnarly, twisted branches. There were many nasty streaks in the trunk showing it had been hit by lightning many times over the years. I wondered how many New England winters it had endured. I looked up through the branches and leaves that reached up into the sky that provided shelter for many birds and squirrels and shade for whoever passed by on a sunny day in August. I thought of how lucky I was to meet this man so many years ago and how he had added substantially to my life.

A few days later we learned of the passing of Rev. Moon at the age of 92. I went back to that park with Ursula to walk and meditate. As we strolled through the park I was drawn to the old tree I had noticed before and discovered that it had been cut down! The only thing remaining was the huge stump. I looked down at the stump in awe. The tree, though old, had seemed healthy just a few days before. There were so many concentric rings in the freshly cut wood. I wondered how old the tree was. I slowly counted the rings. There were exactly 92.

Tree stump in Elm Park, Worcester

On the bright side our son, Michael, did quite well all through high school and is now in the process of applying to some of the most prestigious engineering schools in the country. He is doing his high school internship at a prominent local university at the geophysics lab, testing equipment used in the space program by NASA and Space X. He is well adjusted and has many friends and is always on the go. Ursula and I are working. Our days are full and challenging. We are keeping the dream alive one day at a time with faith, love and a few good friends.

> *To dream the impossible dream*
> *To fight the unbeatable foe*
> *To bear with unbearable sorrow*
> *To run where the brave dare not go*
>
> *To right the unrightable wrong*
> *To love pure and chaste from afar*
> *To try when your arms are too weary*
> *To reach the unreachable star*
>
> "The Impossible Dream"

ABOUT THE AUTHOR

Mark Hanlon is a teacher, traveler, activist, and musician. He graduated from UMass Lowell and earned a master's in religious education from the Unification Theological Seminary. Hanlon has been director of the Unification Church in six states and has led teams of missionaries nationwide, teaching directly and through his music. He currently resides in Massachusetts.